K P WEAVER

Copyright © 2021 K P Weaver

First published in Australia in 2021
by Making Magic Happen Academy

www.makingmagichappenacademy.com
www.karenmcdermott.com.au

All rights reserved. No part of this book may be used or reproduced by any means, graphic, electronic, or mechanical, including photocopying, recording, taping or by any information storage retrieval system without the written permission of the copyright owner except in the case of brief quotations embodied in critical articles and reviews.

Editor: Teena Raffa-Mulligan
Cover and interior design: Ida Jansson

National Library of Australia Cataloguing-in-Publication data:
The Law of Love/Making Magic Happen Academy
Success/Self-help

ISBN (sc): 978-0-6453359-4-1

*"All you need is love,
love is all you need."*

JOHN LENNON

CONTENTS

Introduction   7

My Love Philosophy	12
What Does Love Mean to You?	15
The Law of Love	18
Why Love?	22
Sending Love Ahead	26
Unconditional Love	31
Connecting to Divine Love Source Exercise	35
Everything Grows Through Love	41
Lead With Love	45
Winnie the Pooh Love	49
The Greatest Love of All - the Love Affair with Ourselves.	52
Why is it important to unconditionally love ourselves?	54
Heal Through Love	57
Platonic Love – Plato and love	60
Forbidden love	63
Einstein on Love	67
Marianne Williamson on Love	72

Louise Hay on Love	77
Love and Success	82
Love and Relationships	88
Loving Energy as Your Super Fuel	93
A Love Fuelled Experience	97
BONUS CHAPTER: The Answer is LOVE	103
CONTRIBUTORS	111
Cliona O'Hara	113
Kim Oakhill	115
Taryn Claire	125
Patricia Lovell	129
Leanne Murner	138
About Karen Weaver	*145*
About The Alchemy of Life Magic Series	*146*
References	*148*

INTRODUCTION

I am a great believer that love conquers all. The energy of love is so pure and powerful beyond comprehension that we sometimes limit the possibility of what we can make happen in our lives by accessing our unlimited supply of this golden nectar of life.

One thing I know for sure is that whenever I put loving energy into something it always has the best-case scenario results. Love is the answer; it heals all and loving energy fuels all. We need to know this. We need to embrace it. We need to understand that love is a superpower. Embrace it, harness it, use it. It never runs out; the more you use, the more is created.

Love ripples out. Love connects. By embracing the power of loving energy, we can first change our personal world and as a consequence have an impact on the world in which we live.

In this book I will share insights on different aspects of love. It is important to note that these are my life principles, my philosophy of life that I have gathered through experience and collected wisdoms. I navigate all of the universal laws so that I can live my best possible life. Loving energy is the fuel I use and the success I have had is absolute proof that when you show up and pursue your heart's desire fuelled with love, there are no limits to what you can achieve.

We need more people living with love and let's see our world change. It starts with us and then it ripples out to those around us and beyond. Invest in loving yourself first and others second. It is that important. It is that simple. Don't overcomplicate it.

All of the great minds understood the power of the energy of love. Albert Einstein knew the energy of love. In fact, he wrote a letter to his daughter about it, explaining its power. This demonstrates how smart minds embrace love because they know its potential.

This energetic vibration can be likened to being superhuman; it will make amazing things happen in your life. The world needs more of us embracing this power so we can experience the benefits. Amazing things come through love—family, relationships, passion, healing, wealth, all of the good stuff. Take a moment to think about how many things a day you receive through love, either from yourself or someone else.

Think about what you could add to that list. What could you add to love? There's nothing like that deep, deep connection that happens when you truly love someone. It's the energetic exchange that happens between two people, between parent and child, or between friends or colleagues. There all different types of love, different frequencies of love, but they all come from the same space: genuine intention to connect with somebody else.

It takes courage to love. You cannot love without being hurt, without having courage. Living life with an open heart makes you more susceptible to having a broken heart because love can hurt. Love with expectation will not get you the results you want, and that can be really scary for some people. But I always encourage everyone to love, unconditionally and without expectation of return, because when you love without expectation, you can't be disappointed.

You're just sharing love for the sake of sharing love. Only good things can happen through that. If someone's not ready to receive it, it's sad but it's not your problem. Give it anyway, whether or not you get the response you hoped for, because, believe me, it has had an impact on them. They may not have been ready to receive the love at that moment, but it will sit with them and they will receive it. And when they do, they may not even reach out to you but it had an impact.

Even a smile is a loving gesture. It's sharing love and can change someone's day. At my local shop there was a woman stocking shelves right where I wanted to get something. I went up and said, "Hello, how are you going?" and gave her a big smile. I make sure to do that quite often without expectation of any response whatsoever.

Her demeanour absolutely elevated. It was as if she opened up, her actual physicality opened up, and she smiled. She smiled back and said, "I'm going really good. Thank you. I hope you are too."

I was grateful for her response because it was lovely. My message is clear: give love without expectation.

Even the geniuses of this world understood the value of love and how the universal laws embrace love. Love is fuel. Love is the driving force. Love is immaculate. It is divine, it is eternal, and there is no lack of it. The more we give, the more is created. So embrace love when you can.

Love conquers all.

*I am a decisive person;
I follow through and support
myself with love*

MY LOVE PHILOSOPHY

When I think about love I think more than an intimate relationship with my partner I see a powerful pure energy that when channelled towards something will make it manifest to it highest potential. It's simple to navigate in theory but in practice it can get complicated.

- If you want a great relationship channel love into it,
- If you want more money, love money so much and don't feel shameful about it.
- If you want success in your business channel loving energy into every interaction you make

- If you want connection with your children, love then unconditionally not materialistically.
- If you want magic to happen in your life, believe in infinite possibilities with all of your heart.

These are a few examples of how to navigate love in our lives, you can easily add to this list. They may seem like simple statements, don't they? Yet we make it so complicated in practice. Love is all powerful, it is the divine energy that governs all of the laws, when navigated well it can make all of your heart's desires come to fruition and in turn love will ripple out to those around you and beyond. It can transcend oceans and quantum fields, love is almighty. You will hear me mention this many times in this book, that is because I want it to embed into your heart and mind because in the words of John Lennon, all we need is love, love is all we need!

Your love equation:
open heart + emotional flow + focused energy
= highest potential

Love is such an important principle. One that as humans we often neglect, abuse, or take for granted. Love is supposed to be simple. We just make it complicated because it often originates in our heart and our emotions can run high with it. Yet if we knew that we could leverage our emotions to supercharge our results we would put more effort into this universal governance.

I called this book The Law of Love because I know that entwined through all the universal laws that govern our lives (knowingly or unknowingly) Love is there fuelling everything should we choose it helping us find our way to the best results. Choose love always.

*Sprinkle a bit of love on anything
and it will grow beyond belief.*

WHAT DOES LOVE MEAN TO YOU?

It's really important to recognise what your definition of love is. Think about how you perceive it now and compare that to how you see it when you finish reading this book.

It will help you to connect with the essence of the energy of love and it will also gift you faster access to it when you want to apply it to a scenario in your life.

Whether it be romantic or practical, your definition of love is personal and is always right, just for you.

My definition of love before reading this book is:

_____
_____
_____
_____
_____
_____
_____

My definition of love after reading this book is:

_____
_____
_____
_____
_____
_____
_____

I know that when I learn to love myself first, I can love others better.

THE LAW OF LOVE

Understanding that love is the purest form of energy and a power that we all have the instant ability to access can be a bit overwhelming for some people. I've talked many times about it being an infinite well that we can access at any time, and it is! We often get hurt in life and shield ourselves from love when in fact it is in those moments that we need to bask more in it. Some people unconsciously lock it away because of fear due to the things that have happened in their past and their vulnerability when they open up their hearts and share love.

We're all gifted that infinite supply of love should we choose to embrace it. But what are we to do with that infinite well of love?

We will all experience challenges in life and that means we are evolving. We will all have life lessons to endure that will sink our heart to the pit of our stomach and we may feel like we will never recover, but guess what, you will! When we fuel loving energy into the harsh moments just as we do into the exciting success-driven ones, then we will feel nurtured through every occurrence we endure in life.

Here I share something from Wikipedia because the "pure energy" it talks about is Love. It is an interesting perspective that love and the Universal laws are largely based on the user having faith in the practice, and yet the results far outweigh any questions asked.

In the New Thought spiritual movement, the **Law of Attraction** *is a pseudoscience based on the belief that positive or negative thoughts bring positive or negative experiences into a person's life. The belief is based on the ideas that people and their thoughts are made from "pure energy" and that a process of like energy attracting like energy exists through which a person can improve their health, wealth, and personal relationships. …* **Wikipedia**

Loving energy works in the way we want it to; it is there to serve us, so when we learn how to use it properly we will create one of the most impactful habits that will hold us in good stead for a lifetime. And the great thing is, there is a never-ending supply so you can share love freely in the knowledge that it will never dry up.

We must understand deeply that we must serve ourselves first and others after. When we serve ourselves first it means that others will get the best of us. Let me emphasise that. We are not here to sacrifice all of ourselves. We are here on this world to actually experience joy and through that joy to show up on life and have the best lives possible.

To truly work in alignment with the Law of Love we must choose love first! It must be our first response to everything, even the negative things because those scenarios are more in need of love than others.

We're not here to suffer. Contrary to everybody's belief, we can have our best lives possible if we choose to do so. So why suffer? Why, oh why is sacrifice put on a pedestal? We're not here to sacrifice ourselves. We are here to love ourselves and love one another and we can. That's what brings goodness into the world. When we serve ourselves first, we don't have any scarcity. We don't have any fears of lack. We only have love and quite often that is more than enough.

Choose love always!

"Love is the most powerful force in the universe; it is the only frequency that can transcend all time and space. It's literally all around us like oxygen."

BOB PROCTOR.

WHY LOVE?

When we learn how to open our heart and love with all of ourself, we can make anything happen. Loving energy is the most powerful energy of all; it heals, it grows, it radiates through us and from us and when we choose love instead of fear, that is when the true magic of life can be experienced.

Connect with the love within exercise:

Did you know that love is an actual physical thing that you can gauge? You can identify when absolute divine love is flowing through you as it will feel like a physical surge through your heart. If you haven't connected to it as source energy the best way to do so is through a meditation.

When you learn how to connect with the loving energy source within you it will become more and more accessible when you are manifesting.

Loving energy is a super fuel when it comes to manifesting our desires.

1. Find a place where you feel peace.
2. Take a quiet moment and close your eyes.
3. Allow your mind time to settle and focus in on your heart organ.
4. Listen to the loving energy meditation or follow these words:

Your mind is an explorer on a quest to find the epitome of a pure loving energy source deep within you. It starts at your toes. Hold it there for a moment and feel how it glows right at the centre of your toe. It then slowly makes its way into your foot and begins to navigate through your body. It feels like a warm glow traveling through you. You can feel it deep at the centre of your being as it continues to travel past your ankle and up your leg right past your knee and slowly makes its way up to your groin, through your pelvic area and holds space in your tummy area, where you process nourishment. You feel full. And then it happens, it moves a little more upwards and lands in your heart. You feel its warmth as it surges through your heart with palpitations to let you know it beats only for you. Feel deeply as those palpations surge love through your veins. Know in this moment what it is like to feel divine love. The divine love that is always stored deep within you and that you can access any time. Know the power of this divine energy and how it can change any negative to a positive. Loving energy conquers all. Use it for your soul's purpose. Sit still in that energy for a moment and when you are ready, let your love seed travel up through your chest area, igniting you as it flows through to your throat where love- filled words will flow through, and up through your head to your mind where it has now created a special compartment for you to store and access this loving energy when you so wish. Loving energy is limitless, there is no end, the more you use the more it creates, it is infinite and so are you. Know your power and the power of the love within you.

5. Once you have harnessed the divine loving energy within you, you will be able to access it when you need to, to super charge any endeavour or connection.
6. Know that when you do something with loving intention you have given your best to any scenario and so you can show up authentically you.

Let everything you do be done through love.

I must give myself the best, in order to be my best for others.

SENDING LOVE AHEAD

Sending love ahead. Think about it for a moment. It's such a simple concept and yet so many people don't do it. Then there are others who do it without even realising it. I have lots of examples to share with you from my own personal endeavours. I could do it so much more than I do.

When you set the intention in it, it's much more powerful and when you do it constantly and consistently, it becomes part of your DNA. So learn to do it and wait till you see the results. You will live a more harmonious life, a life filled with loving responses when you send love ahead. For example, if you're going for a big job, or if you set an intention and you've acted on an inspired thought, or if you've had an argument with a loved one and you really want your next interaction to be more amicable.

There were times when I had an argument with my husband and he would go to work and yes, he would have time to stew on it and he believed that he was right. I would hold the anger, the frustration and the stubbornness within me towards our argument because I believed that I was right. Both of us were so passionate about our stances and not meeting in the middle to find a level playing field.

The energy within both of us was so powerful that you could actually feel it, even though he was 100 kilometres away and had a job. Then one day I when I started awakening, I thought, I'm going to try something and see if it works. I never told him or anybody else. I think I was pregnant at the time.

I thought, *OK, I know I want to be right. I know this is really important to me, but obviously there's something within him that's very important to him. So I'm willing to explore a solution together.* I sent love ahead and it was a different person who came home from work that day after what may have been days of not speaking to each other. It was amazing.

And yes, maybe my demeanour had changed and I understand that. But I honestly know that sending love ahead helped the situation 100 percent. In another example, I set an intention that I really wanted to get my books into the US and I had an inspired thought that I actioned. I sent books to a big publisher. Big risk, you know, big thing, so I sent them with love.

When I knew they had arrived, I followed up with an email and introduced myself, saying I knew it was a bit cheeky to do so. I got a really awesome reply, because in my emails I send love through them to the receiver and they can feel that, without a doubt. I'm sending love ahead and the replies I get are more connected.

Sending love works. So how do we do it? What are the strategies? One, you sit in the scenario, whether it be something you want to achieve or something you want to heal. Whatever it is, you sit in the energy of the ideal scenario of that. It is really powerful and really important that you sit in the energy of it and send love into it.

You will see the results and whatever you might think, there's no questioning results. I don't overthink it. I just embrace it. It works. You can actually physically heal someone by sending love ahead and this is especially powerful when people come together in a collective to send loving, healing energy to a source of ill health.

Self-help author and lecturer Bob Proctor teaches that diseases and ill health are when your body is not at ease. When we send love ahead, that's right at a target. Whether it be a country, a town or an individual, they all receive that energy because energy can be like a sonic boom. It propels across many, many miles to reach where it needs to go, because when you target energy at a single source, it receives it.

Similar to the way we can contact someone by phone on the other side of the world in an instant, we humans are energy transmitters. Whenever we target something or someone and send love, it will be received. It is all the more powerful when the receiver knows it's coming because they're open to receiving the transmission but it doesn't have to necessarily be that way.

Try the concept of the three-step strategy. One, sit in the energy. Sit in the moment to connect with your heart centre.

You can use the loving energy meditation I shared to really connect with your heart centre where you can compile a ball of that loving essence. You know how powerful that energy is and you can project it to where it is needed. Remember, it's not as if it's going to dry up.

The more you use it, the more you're going to have. OK, you can use it on others, on yourself, on a scenario, but whatever it is, just use it for good because love conquers all. Love is all. God is love. We are love. The more we embrace love, the more goodness we and others can experience. The third step of that process after you compile the love is to really target it, to send it where it needs to go. Feel the love with all your heart and just catapult it to where it needs to go, and smile.

Be grateful that you have that love to give. Please know that you are so powerful, more powerful than you can ever know. I have done this and if I can do it, you can do it. We all have the same abilities and we just need to access them. When you learn how to unlock your infinite well of love, anything can happen. Enjoy!

Love life and it will love you back

UNCONDITIONAL LOVE

One thing I can say for certain is that love has played a big part in my life. I have been blessed enough to know unconditional love from the day I was born. If you are reading this and don't have a foundation of unconditional love from your childhood, don't worry. It might take a little effort but you will be able to capture and apply it to your future from now. It can become a habit from any age, as it's a choice to behold the mindful practice of identifying when you have experienced unconditional love in your life and treasure each moment of it.

I know that I was born from that beautiful connection between two people who so wanted a child to love. That is one of the most beautiful essences to be borne from and I do feel truly blessed. True, such love, they never take it for granted.

Have you ever thought about the essence of the love that you were borne from? I remember my sister talking about her IVF journey. She had been through three IVF journeys and on her third one, she knew it was going to be successful because when the embryo was implanted, she saw a light flash. She knew in that moment. I get goose bumps every time I think of it. True pure life. Implanted and getting ready to be born. Oh, it just gives me shivers.

As much as loving, intimate connections with our family, our partners and our children is important, the energy of love is forever flowing through us, around us, and entangling in every aspect of our lives. Loving energy is so much more than an interaction between two people. It is an absolutely amazing relationship with the whole of humanity and the universe. When we are opened and we live through love, where we choose to see the best in people, when we choose to show off the best of ourselves and do the work that we need to do in ourselves so that we can be the best for others, it is so powerful.

It is so powerful that you cannot mistake it for anything else, you just feel it. There's nothing like the feeling of true love. Love for yourself. Love for your life. Love for others. Because through that love, you always want the best. You always want the best outcome for everyone involved, not just for yourself. You don't live life as a selfish endeavour, you live life with the best outcome in mind, not just for you, but for everyone.

That is how the law works. We need more people living through the law of love. We need more people honouring love, not fearing it. So many people fear love yet love is to be embraced, love is to be shared, love is to be celebrated because love conquers all. It allows us to grow, to heal, to evolve, to connect, to make this world a better place for now and for future generations.

It is the most important aspect of all humanity. We need to learn how to love, how to love with an open heart, not just how to love with one person. We need to open our minds when it comes to love, because when we do, we change things, we change people, we change our world. We make amazing things happen. Miracles happen because of love, love, love. It needs to be embraced because it makes the world a better place.

I pursue my goals with loving intention.

CONNECTING TO DIVINE LOVE SOURCE EXERCISE

To connect to love you will need to find stillness. In this busy bee world we now live in, it can be tough to access love straight away. If you do not already have an automatic tendency to go to love when acting or reacting then you will need to rewire your heart and mind.

It will be tougher for some people than others. I highly recommend that you visit the work of Louise Hay or other wonderful love motivated philosophers so that you can get into the headspace of connecting to that energy. It will open your mind to the possibility and make it easier for you to tap into it.

Please know that you might start to have a physical response to this. I did when I reconnected.

I have shared in the past that I thought that there was something wrong with my heart because I was experiencing erratic heart flutters. They scared me, and I even ended up on a heart monitor. I was very much a mum at home all of the time and quite out of the blue a friend asked me if I would like to join her for a meditation at another woman's home nearby. It was quite intimate, just four of us, and I had never meditated before so it was new to me. I just knew that something was calling me. Little did I know that I was to experience a moment that would change my life.

We relaxed into our chairs and the lady played a meditation tape which featured the voice of a man from an eastern culture. It was quite off-putting at first but I rolled with it. It took a few minutes but I relaxed into it as he led us through focal points in our body, first starting at our toes and moving upwards. When he came to our heart, he spoke about feeling the love our heart has in abundance and how we can break the layer we have covered it in, allowing it to shatter so that we can love freely, and through love everything grows. Well, in that very moment my heart fluttered so much that my cheeks flushed, and I identified it to be the same heart flutter that had been concerning me enough to go to my doctor who had put me on a heart monitor for a day. The realisation that I ignited this reaction changed me. Tears of relief streamed down my cheeks and I knew that my heart flutters were nothing to fear. They were in fact something to embrace and action, something that I could use to grow the love in my life, and at that time it was self-love I needed most as I was pouring so much into my beautiful family but not myself. It had never occurred to me that you can't pour from an empty cup and from then on, I ensured that I took time to refill my cup. Going to this meditation itself was pouring into my cup as I had a six-week-old who I would never have left for a moment before; and you know what, she survived and we had more fulfilling hugs on my return.

One other thing happened that night that I must share before I finish this story. At first when we came out of the meditation, I said nothing but the group had felt the pulsating energy radiating from me so I told them about my self-discovery. We then went on to tap into a message for each other my immediate thought was *Oh no, I'm not going to be able to do this*, but I tried. When I tapped into the energy of the lady I was to get a message for, my ear began hurting badly with a sharp stabbing pain that was so distinct I couldn't ignore it, and a message came through that healing was in motion. I relayed what I felt and thought and it turned out her grandson was experiencing really bad ear infections and they were all worried.

I share the latter because when messages come through us for others it can really help so we should not keep them to ourselves. We just share and let them do what is needed with the message. That too is love in motion and can make a huge difference. I have on many occasions activated an inspired thought that has come into my heart and mind for someone, and I share without worrying that they might think I am crazy. It may not make sense in that moment but it will later on to them, and I often get a message back saying, "Remember you told me this, well…" Yes, that takes courage and for inhibitions to be in check.

So how will you tap into your divine love source? Follow the steps below to help you ignite your divine love source and it will become increasingly easier to access it.

STEP 1

Expose yourself to a loving energy source higher than you normally experience by listening to someone who encompasses love always.

STEP 2

Trust that love can hold you.

STEP 3

Find a way to consciously connect to your loving light source every day. Make it a habit.

STEP 4

When faced with a challenge, choose love first in your response.

STEP 5

Be love. Understand that those who fear love's potential don't need you to shield yourself, they need you to shine it on them so that they might free their own light.

STEP 6

Love deeper, love more, love yourself, love unconditionally.

Once you experience divine love and know that you have the power to access it when you choose to, that is a powerful realisation and there is no going back from that point. There is your life before that moment and your life afterwards and there is a significant divide between them.

"*Love is the most important
healing power there is.*"

LOUISE L. HAY

EVERYTHING GROWS THROUGH LOVE

The law of love. When we pour love into something, it grows, whether we do so consciously or subconsciously. When we tap into that loving energy, whatever is the recipient of that will grow. I want to give you a quirky little story about my hair, and it's just an example. You can apply this to more serious things, such as a connection with someone, getting a job, saving someone's life, healing someone.

I used to always get my hair done every week and it was always so healthy with a beautiful shine. I love my hair and I did this religiously. It was something I did for myself so obviously I was pouring love into my hair and it was benefiting and showing vibrancy. Happy hair!

When we moved to Australia, I was 35 weeks pregnant with my third child. Getting my hair done wasn't a priority on my list and of course I didn't have my regular hairdresser. Twelve years later, I started taking care of my hair again and every few months I'd go to the hairdresser's and get my hair blow dried but I couldn't justify the cost of having a colour or any other treatment.

Then it got to the stage where the business was going well so I decided to take every Thursday morning for me. The first thing on my agenda was to go and get my hair blow dried at 9 am every week. You know, I could blow dry it at home, but it never looks or feels the same. Taking that time out to sit and get something done for me is important to me, and it makes me feel good so I started booking in. Then I got a colour done at the hairdresser's and started getting six-weekly trims.

I had become used to thinking that my hair was not like it used to be and wishing that it would grow and that it was thicker. Yes, I know the power of thoughts, but sometimes you can't help yourself. And then suddenly I noticed that *Wow, my hair is getting thicker. Wow, my hair is getting longer. Wow, my hair looks and feels so healthy.* My kids were starting to notice it too, and they were saying, "Oh, Mommy's hair is so soft and so healthy."

I've been taking the time and giving some self-love to myself and to my hair that is actually important to me, so I've been reaping the rewards and I did it unconsciously.

If you just take a moment to stop and allow yourself to pour your love into something that matters to you, you see the benefits of it in many other ways. With my hair so much healthier I look better on camera so on Thursdays I schedule in making videos. That's become my video day. I'm more productive, more confident on video and I'm getting more contacts due to being more visible, which is attracting many more opportunities my way, all because I made the conscious decision to pour love into my hair.

I wasn't feeling good about my hair and this was blocking my mind from progressing. Think about what is blocked around you because you're not pouring love into some element of you. Ask yourself what matters to you, because what matters to you is important not only for you but for those around you. It's important for your business too, because when you pour love into yourself and what matters to you, everyone and everything benefits. It has a knock-on effect.

If something is calling and wants you to give more to it, stop and take the time to pour love into it, because the benefits will far outweigh any time commitment or financial sacrifice. Pour love into things and watch them grow.

When I live through love,
everyone benefits.

LEAD WITH LOVE

I have been observing (and contributing) to a new type of leadership that is surging forward in our world. The inspired leader. These leaders are mission focused on making the world a better place, they see the bigger picture, they understand that there is no one size fits all approach to leadership, and being a leader is a privilege not an accolade. They show up even when the harsh leaders fear their strength and so try to knock them down. They lead with loving intention and know the power of connection, unity and bringing people together.

They are not afraid to share how they do things, it's not a secret to be them, it is a choice. This inspired leadership comes from leading by example, putting yourself in front, being courageous and most importantly being kind. An inspired leader never brings someone down to elevate themselves. An inspired leader rises higher by connecting wider with others, their agenda is aligned with their passion for having a positive impact on the world and it will be fused with their interests so that they can continue to fill their cup as they grow.

I believe this is a perfect blend of giving and receiving. We see many humanitarians giving so much of themselves that they end up sick or depleted, whereas a dictator or controlling leader thinks only of their own agenda and what they believe to be the right thing to do is always filling their own cup. An inspired leader considers all aspects of the decision, especially the balance between the desired outcome and the emotional toll and they know the importance of keeping themselves well so that they can serve at the highest capacity.

To lead with love inspired leaders embrace kindness and use it as a super power to move forward. Kindness is embedded deep in love and when we are kind we are also loving, so in turn we are leading through love.

New Zealand Prime Minister Jacinda Ardern is a great example of a leader who I believe leads with love. She doesn't shy away from the big decisions and has the courage to be kind. I loved watching how she led her country through a terrorist attack and also the global pandemic.

She ignores the call to be harsher in her navigation of her leadership. Even though what she has had to put in place may have felt harsh, she has delivered the solution with kindness and knowledge and has in turn inspired other nations to see the strength in this type of leadership so her nation responds well to her decisions because they feel part of the solution.

I am encouraged to see that there are so many more leaders in our world embracing loving values in their actions moving forward. This virtuous approach to leadership puts people at ease and helps to build trust within nations, within suburbs, within homes, within our hearts. It has a ripple effect from widespread to personal.

Let's all embrace a more loving approach to the way we lead.

Loving energy is the most powerful energy of all. If you want to attract something into your life, love it!

WINNIE THE POOH LOVE

One of the most endearing characters that my family and I love is Winnie the Pooh. He may be mistaken for a sloth-like persona, but he is far from it, for his mind is fuelled by love and many of his expressions are deeply rooted in the universal law of love. Pooh's delivery is always extremely relaxed and he has captured the hearts of generations of children and adults alike. *Winnie the Pooh* published in 1926, was the first book in the series. Author AA Milne used this adorable bear to help us to see what love would do in any scenario. Even though we will all face challenges in life there is always a loving solution. It is important to get some little insight into the person behind the character because hidden depths can be discovered.

Winnie the Pooh helps us to see ourselves through loving eyes. He says, *"You are braver than you believe, stronger than you seem and smarter than you think. But the most important thing is: even if we are apart, I will always be with you."*

This is a reminder that we are so much more than we will ever give ourselves credit for and sometimes we need to believe in ourselves a little more so that we can be the best version of ourselves. No matter if someone is on our side there is always someone's love in our heart to embrace.

Winnie the Pooh is our potential subconscious mind, the loving answer, the solution to all our woes, the guiding light that we all have the potential to live through.

Like Winnie the Pooh I believe that we all make life way too complicated. Although I don't aspire to live life at Pooh's pace I do understand the analogy of being in the pursuit of what fulfills us. His pursuit of honey was the one purpose that gave him much joy and took him on new adventures every day. He never knew where the honey would be but he had faith that he would find it when he needed it and didn't let much stop him from getting it as he overcame all obstacles with courage and love.

Pooh Bear never apologises or explains his passion for honey and although it gets him in lots of sticky situations he continues to move forward in love and kindness in pursuit of his goal. Pooh knows the journey will never be smooth but it will be an adventure because he embraces all of the lessons he learns along the way and he brings his friends along for the journey. We can learn a lot from that.

No matter what your 'honey' is, pursue it with loving intention and never give up!

*I know that LOVE is
the highest power of all.*

THE GREATEST LOVE OF ALL - THE LOVE AFFAIR WITH OURSELVES.

The greatest love story of all is the love we have for ourselves. As a hopeless romantic I have learned the power of self-love, not in an egotistical 'I love myself' way but in the 'I am working with the divine energy of the universe' type of love. Love is the most productive energy of all. The vibration is so high that it can transcend dimensions and physical distance. If you tune into a loving frequency sent by a loved one, you can reap the benefits even if they are on the other side of the world.

I have to face the reality that being a mum of six and owning three publishing houses is busy but I like to take it in my stride as much as possible. A blend that I find works for me is to work throughout school terms and shift into a more relaxed mindset during school holidays when I have fun with my kids by day and I do some work in the early morning and evening if needed. I switch back into work mode after the school holidays.

Right now my kids have just finished their Term 3 holidays and so this present school term is all about getting ahead for me because their next holiday break will be six weeks over the summer. To make it productive for me I write during this time. We have a big backyard and I set up an outdoor desk for me and for them. It's so good for the soul. I have been doing this for five years and it works so I roll with it. My kids are getting older and when it comes to a time to transition this arrangement I will but for now I wouldn't change it for the world.

When I am in my work flow and I hit a day of overwhelm I close my diary and head to the beach for a walk. It is my happy place and I adore walking there, being near the ocean is so rejuvenating. I could stay at my desk and push through but that doesn't serve anyone well.

Are there times in your life when you could practise more self-care?

My tips for taking care of you:

1. Prioritise yourself as well as others.
2. If you are feeling overloaded take a break rather than pushing through.
3. It is your responsibility to take care of you.
4. Time for you does not need to be extravagant or pre-planned.
5. Know what your go-to instant recharge is and do more of that.
6. Get outside more and experience nature, it is an instant energy boost.

Why is it important to unconditionally love ourselves?

We cannot hope for others to love us when we don't love ourselves unconditionally. We have the ability to love ourselves unconditionally and through that love create a life that we love to live.

It is important to remember that we are the masters of our own happiness. I see many people hand over the keys to their happiness to someone else and that never works. Happiness is an inside job! Sure, others can make us happy, especially the life partners we choose, but it is our choice to be happy in that moment and to choose that person to share it with us. I am sure that many marriages break down because one partner has bestowed responsibility for their happiness onto the other partner and their expectations have not been met. Being responsible for someone else's happiness is hard work and can lead to resentment or failure and they are not high vibrational energies.

When we have a love affair with ourselves first, we show how we hope to be loved and how we can love another. That attracts the right person into our life, it emits from us like an energy vibration sending signals out that will ensure our heart's desire makes its way to us. Loving yourself first is one of the smartest things you will ever do.

*The most magical moments
are entwined in loving essence.*

HEAL THROUGH LOVE

*"Love is the great miracle cure.
Loving ourselves works miracles in our lives."*
Louise L. Hay.

I cannot speak about healing through love without mentioning the renowned Louise L. Hay. This lady encompassed loving energy, it emitted from every atom in her being. She opened my mind to healing at a whole new level, the healing ability we have within us.

When I experience an illness, discomfort or other physical woe I always ask myself what could be the underlying issue.

As self-help author and lecturer Bob Proctor shared in *The Secret*, disease cannot reside in a body that is in an emotionally balanced state. It may not be comforting to hear but it is interesting to discover that through love we can assist the healing process.

I say assist because I am a great believer that conventional medicine was created by scientists through their love for humanity, so it is an important approach to treating illness but it is not the only way.

It is important that we choose to pour love, not fear, into ourselves or our loved ones who are unwell. Many people go instantly into fear and that is understandable as a diagnosis of serious illness can instigate a shock reaction. However, when we live through love, we can guide ourselves or our loved ones into a more emotionally healing state, one filled with hope. Try to focus on a healthy outcome together and let the doctors deal with the illness, because when an illness consumes your mind as well as your body, healing potential is delayed.

The work of researcher, lecturer and author Dr Joe Dispenza may help navigate you inwards toward the miraculous healing potential that each of us has. His story is phenomenal. He speaks about how you can regenerate and heal at a cellular level.

To find out morfe, visit his website
https://drjoedispenza.com/

I feel love in very essence of my being.

PLATONIC LOVE
– PLATO AND LOVE

Platonic love is a type of love that is not sexual. The term is named after the Greek philosopher Plato, though the philosopher never used the term himself. Platonic love, as devised by Plato, concerns rising through levels of closeness to wisdom and true beauty, from carnal attraction to individual bodies to attraction to souls, and eventually, union with the truth.
Wikipedia

Platonic love is the deep connection we can have with someone else that does not have to be a sexual relationship. Friendship is a deep platonic love and most of us choose our friends because we feel a connection that we embrace without necessarily understanding it. When love isn't questioned the loving can be the main focus. Although I imagine many friends wouldn't consider themselves to be in a loving relationship with each other the energetic exchange is definitely fuelled by love.

According to Plato, the pure energy of love is born into us all and we will always seek someone to make us feel whole. It is natural for us to do so. As we have evolved through the ages women have become more independent and the 'need' for a partner is not for everyone. I have been truly fortunate to have experienced what it is like to be a complete whole alongside someone else. It is a next level experience, one that requires love, trust and co-working to maintain. People continue to marry and in a sense it is a 'two-becoming-one' philosophy.

What about the platonic love? How does that survive?

It survives because the connection is deep. I have made many close friends over the years and sometimes we may not see each other for months or years but when we reconnect, we just pick up where we left off. It's a truly special connection, one that doesn't need explanation, it is just beautiful to behold and celebrate.

"Love is born into every human being; it calls back the halves of our original nature together; it tries to make one out of two and heal the wound of human nature.

Each of us, then, is a 'matching half' of a human whole… and each of us is always seeking the half that matches him."

*Those who are harsh need
more love than others.*

FORBIDDEN LOVE

Take a moment to think forbidden love. It's so alluring and how it intrigues and excites us.

We know it's not good for us, it's not in our best interests. But why do we love it so much? And is it love—or lust? I'd say it's lust because of the excitement and the adrenaline and the newness of it. It's probably not a love we aspire to experience for a lifetime. It won't align with our values.

Aphrodite really intrigues me because she's the goddess of love and fertility, she embodies everything that is love and everybody is attracted to her inner self as much as her beauty. She's as beautiful on the inside as she is on the outside.

Aphrodite epitomises love.

When you're that loving from the inside, it actually shines on the outside and people will see you in that light. We can all put on makeup and make ourselves look beautiful. When love is shining through us and emitting from us that is really beautiful.

Aphrodite was so enticing to everyone because she loved openheartedly. There was no shielding. She was true to the essence of love. She did not apologise for the love she emitted, she embraced loving energy, and so many people gravitated towards that. Aphrodite couldn't be anything else but loving because that's who she was. And why should she change who she was for the comfort of others?

We all have the potential to be that loving, beaming light shine through us. I try to hang out in loving essence as much as possible. It's the most beautiful, pure energy that emits from you. It's just the most beautiful sensation yet not everybody gets to feel that in their lifetime. And that is so sad because we all have the potential to feel it and be that energy source, that energy magnet that attracts amazing people to us.

One of the things that I wanted us all to learn from Aphrodite is don't be afraid to be all loving. Whenever you are love fuelled you have the power over who and what you love, and there is nothing more beautiful than that. We will all evolve through different stages of love in our lifetime; the curiosity of our teenage years, the foundation building in our twenties; and for most the all-encompassing love of having families.

We must embrace the Aphrodite call to love with all of our hearts but ensure we align it with our morals and values, because then we can love openly and passion is an important part of the bond that we have with a life partner.

When in turn that evolves into the creation of a new life, to my heart that is the most special gift of all. For me there's nothing more beautiful than witnessing a pure and loving moment when a mother is sitting with her child in her arms and both their hearts are open. You can feel the pure loving energy being emitted. Not everybody gets to experience it, but for those who do, it's the essence of beauty and pure unconditional love in that tender moment.

What is an Aphrodite moment in your life? When do you shine a beautiful light from within? Do you know that that light shines out of you? People will see and feel that beauty.

I know when I feel it. I've never felt so much flow in my life. I always feel that I'm acting at my highest vibration. All the wonderful things that come my way when I'm in that energy are there because of the energy I'm emitting so take some time to connect with the essence of love within you.

Make a conscious decision to choose love? Choose the loving answer. Choose the loving solution. Sometimes it's just to let things go. Sometimes it's to forgive. Sometimes it's just spending a moment with someone you love instead of rushing around.

Be mindful to choose love when you can and more often than usual. Can you see the difference that is going to make in your life? Be the Aphrodite in your life. Channel your Aphrodite because we all have her within us. Then people will see and experience the beauty that is your inner Aphrodite.

Live through love.

EINSTEIN ON LOVE

I nearly didn't publish the below chapter as when we researched the validity of the letter attached it was never confirmed that it was authentic but for me it really doesn't matter who wrote it. Yes, I love to romanticise that it was Einstein who wrote it to his daughter. However, whoever it was that wrote this letter I absolutely resonate with it and so please indulge me and the essence of what I am sharing.

A few years ago I stumbled across a letter that Einstein wrote to his daughter and I fell in love. I have a huge respect for his work and the era in which his genius reigned. Reading this letter and truly understanding the love equation he is sharing, with the genuine open-hearted connection that any dad has for his daughter to understand a deeper meaning to life, I saw this genius from a whole different angle.

In the letter he talks about the Universal Force of love and how the concept is way beyond the comprehension of the masses of this time. What he wrote may have been before its time then and may still be beyond many people now, especially those who haven't yet awakened.

I have to admit that when I read this letter my heart does a somersault of excitement. I am in love with this letter and the insights it shares. It is not only a love for his daughter that Einstein is expressing here, it is a love for humanity and the hope that one day we will be able to see the light and its potential to heal, grow, and supercharge our potential.

LOVE HAS NO LIMITS! Therefore love is the most powerful force there is, with the most gratifying results!

He speaks on the bomb of love and how it can destroy hate, selfishness and greed.

LOVE is the quintessence of life, it conquers all! Einstein is resolute in the power of love. If only we were all so resolute in it and understood that the more we use from our internal supply, the more we have because love multiplies the more we use it. It is infinite, we can never run out of it.

I invite you to read this letter, more than once. And when you finish, please take a moment to share your thoughts and how you can activate more opportunities to express love in your life.

A letter from Albert Einstein to his daughter, Lieserl on The Universal Force of Love

"When I proposed the theory of relativity, very few understood me, and what I will reveal now to transmit to mankind will also collide with the misunderstanding and prejudice in the world.

I ask you to guard the letters as long as necessary, years, decades, until society is advanced enough to accept what I will explain below.

There is an extremely powerful force that, so far, science has not found a formal explanation to. It is a force that includes and governs all others and is even behind any phenomenon operating in the universe and has not yet been identified by us. This universal force is LOVE.

When scientists looked for a unified theory of the universe, they forgot the most powerful unseen force. Love is Light, that enlightens those who give and receive it. Love is gravity because it makes some people feel attracted to others. Love is power, because it multiplies the best we have, and allows humanity not to be extinguished in their blind selfishness. Love unfolds and reveals. For love we live and die. Love is God and God is Love.

This force explains everything and gives meaning to life. This is the variable that we have ignored for too long, maybe because we are afraid of love because it is the only energy in the universe that man has not learned to drive at will.

To give visibility to love, I made a simple substitution in my most famous equation. If instead of $E = mc^2$, we accept that the energy to heal the world can be obtained through love multiplied by the speed of light squared, we arrive at the conclusion that love is the most powerful force there is, because it has no limits.

After the failure of humanity in the use and control of the other forces of the universe that have turned against us, it is urgent that we nourish ourselves with another kind of energy...

If we want our species to survive, if we are to find meaning in life, if we want to save the world and every sentient being that inhabits it, love is the one and only answer.

Perhaps we are not yet ready to make a bomb of love, a device powerful enough to entirely destroy the hate, selfishness and greed that devastate the planet.

However, each individual carries within them a small but powerful generator of love whose energy is waiting to be released.

When we learn to give and receive this universal energy, dear Lieserl, we will have affirmed that love conquers all, is able to transcend everything and anything, because love is the quintessence of life.

I deeply regret not having been able to express what is in my heart, which has quietly beaten for you all my life. Maybe it's too late to apologise, but as time is relative, I need to tell you that I love you and thanks to you I have reached the ultimate answer!"

Your father,
Albert Einstein

Did this ignite anything within you? A new perspective perhaps?

Everything thrives in love.

MARIANNE WILLIAMSON ON LOVE

A Course in Miracles is a spiritual self-study program designed to awaken us to our oneness with God and Love. Published in 1976 and said to be dictated directly by Christ to its scribe, the course has been translated into more than 20 different languages and remains popular today. I haven't studied it intensively, though I plan to at some stage, but I have delved in and out of it and found it interesting and actionable. Recently I read A Return to Love: Reflections on the Principles of A Course in Miracles by Marianne Williamson, based on the author's experience as a teacher of the study guide. In it she explains how applying the principles of love to all difficulties can aid in healing and bring about a personal transformation of the reader.

One thing that stood out for me in this book was where Williamson talks about how many people strive for happiness, possessions, ambitions or goals. She says we should all strive for peace because no matter what we achieve, no matter what our goals are, no matter what our essence of life is that we want, it all leads back to peace, because when we're happy, we're at peace in our hearts. This resonates with me because I always prioritise joy in my life, and joy and happiness obviously go hand in hand.

On deeper reflection, I realised that yes, being joyful brings me peace and harmony in my heart, and that got me thinking more on a world-wide scale because with love comes peace. In our world there is so much warfare between countries and dissension between individuals. Injecting love into those situations can bring us back to peace but that's a long journey, especially when there are brick walls of fear and anger. The only way to conquer those is through love and loving intention.

I come from Northern Ireland and I remember the peace process. I was actually part of it in a small way, because when the peace process was being embraced or trialled, at least in Northern Ireland, there was still going to be a family history of all the terrible things that had happened throughout the conflicts.

But people didn't want the warfare and unnecessary loss of life to continue for their children so they put some things on pause to see how a peace process would work. They didn't do it so much for themselves as for future generations, which was wonderful. As part of the peace-building process, there was an amazing initiative by Smashing Times in collaboration with the University of Dublin to give people an opportunity to express their emotions and find solutions through the safe space of drama.

I went through the application process and was accepted for the program, which was fully funded, so for a whole year we went to different locations all around Ireland and Northern Ireland for a weekend once a month. It was an intensive program of workshops, guest speakers, drama classes and conflict resolution and at the end we had to put together and present our own stage productions.

I was an actress in lipstick, powder and politics. Now I don't have the best memory but I remembered my lines and got into character and achieved my acting goal. The initiative was an amazing experience, and after it ended we all went off into our respective arenas.

I taught drama in art centres and mental health organisations and also tutored first year college students. I was using the drama module with the peace building initiatives in it and oh my goodness, the results were huge. It was amazing to watch people connect through drama, through that safe space where they had permission to express without consequence. It was so therapeutic for them, so very powerful, and if strong emotions were triggered through the drama exercises, we were trained to manage that.

As Marianne Williamson says, we should prioritise peace. It may not be a sexy word, but it is fundamental to healing our societies. When we have peace, we are surrounded by love. When we have peace, we are able to facilitate love, and love is the highest energy of all. It's in our best interest to facilitate peace because then love can flow freely through and around us.

The more love we have, the more love we can create, and loving energy helps us to live abundant lives. Loving energy helps us fulfil our dreams. With only eight percent of the population of the world living their dream, we need to increase that number through love and know peace. And I adore that thought and the prospect of embracing peace, which I will be doing from here on in.

We need to make peace a sexy word and start consciously making peace. Peace is achievable for all our societies across the world. We need to believe in the possibilities that can come from peace, the power of it.

Let's incorporate peace into our very DNA, into our very thought processes. Let's aspire to have peace in everything that we do and everything we aspire to, because when we have peace, we have love. There is no higher energy than love. Love is the provider. Love is the cherisher and love will ensure that we have enough for all and that no one is left without.

Know that those who hurt you are probably the ones who need your love the most but keep your heart strong by putting on your love-filled super shield first; nothing can penetrate that!

LOUISE HAY ON LOVE

When I first discovered Louise Hay, I read her *I Love Myself* affirmation many times. I actually printed it out and read it like a prayer. There is something about going into that divine energy space that dusts away all negativity and you are comforted by something that is almighty. The realisation that we have a love within us that can eradicate any negative energy that surrounds us is both gentle and beautiful but oh so very powerful.

I discovered *You Can Heal Your Life* by Louise Hay at the same time I discovered *The Secret* by Rhonda Byrne. Both shared the power and influence our minds have in manifesting our future but what made me resonate with Louise Hay is that she helped me to open my heart and stop shielding it. I hadn't realised I had shielded it so much even though I lived life with an open heart. As with many other people, over time as we endure heartache and betrayal and life in general, we subconsciously create a protective shield around our heart and the light force within us dulls.

It takes courage to live life with an unshielded heart but what I realised and what I want everyone reading this to realise is that our heart may be perceived to be soft and tender but it is actually one of the strongest organs in our body. Physically it works every nanosecond to keep us alive by pumping blood through our veins and it is also an endless energy source that when allowed to expand and contract freely it will make the impossible possible, our desires reality and our outer world brighter.

Louise Hay created a beautiful space where she could show up and host others through their awakening process, a gentle love fuelled space to hold us until our love shone through. A place where we could retreat into a beautiful energy and refuel. Her loving well was ever flowing and everyone who experienced her loving sanctuary would benefit. She believed there was goodness within everyone, they only needed guidance to find it and the support to help it grow to a point where it could sustain them and continue to grow. Since her death Louise Hay's legacy lives on and her books filled with philosophies and wisdom are timeless and will continue to help others through their awakening.

As Hay says in the affirmation poem below, we all have an infinite well of love and when we allow it to come to the surface there is an endless supply to pour from.

Please visit my website to access a heart opening free meditation that will help you unshield your heart so that you can feel the true potential of the love within you.

"Deep at the centre of my being, there is an infinite well of love.

I now allow this love to flow to the surface.

It fills my heart, my body, my mind, my consciousness, my very being, and radiates out from me in all directions and returns to me multiplied.

The more love I use and give, the more I have to give.

The supply is endless.

It is an expression of my inner joy.

I love myself;

Therefore, I take loving care of my body.

I lovingly feed it,

I lovingly groom it and dress it, and my body lovingly responds to me with vibrant health and energy.

I love myself;

Therefore, I behave and think in a loving way to all people,

For I know that that which I give out returns to me multiplied.

I only attract loving people in my world, for they are a mirror of what I am.

I love myself;

Therefore, I forgive and totally release the past and all past experiences.

I am free.

I love myself;

Therefore, I live totally in the now,

Experiencing each moment as good and knowing that my future is bright and joyous and secure,

For I am a beloved child of the Universe,

And the Universe lovingly takes care of me,

Now and forever more."

© Louise Hay

*The energy of love triumphs all worry,
all fear, all questioning, all time, all space.
It has no beginning, and no end.
Love lives forevermore.*

ADREA PETERS, QUANTUM LOVE.

LOVE AND SUCCESS

There is no more powerful energy that you can put into the pursuit of your success than love. When we do things with loving intention, people can feel it. They end up supporting us more on our quest and they can see the passion, the flame within us burning with the desire of what we want to achieve.

Napoleon Hill's book *Think and Grow Rich* took twenty-five years to research and write. This book is a labour of love. Can you imagine that much of your life being dedicated to collecting and analysing stories from people across the world? This book has now become the foundation of so many success strategies worldwide. If you're going to do anything for yourself and your success journey, whether it's in pursuit of the perfect career, in entrepreneurship or anything else, you need to read, this book.

Bob Proctor who owned Procter Gamble Institute studied Think and Grow Rich for fifty years. He studied it every day, dropping in and out of it. It's a book that I want engraved within my knowledge bank because every time I read or listen to it, something else resonates. Hill's premise is that *your thoughts, whether positive or negative, become your reality. You must control your thoughts if you want to control your destiny.* A foundation has developed around the book and there are now many people associated with delivering its teachings and their perspectives on the principles it presents. It is one of the books on the reading list that you'll find at the back of this book.

We all learn from each other. Napoleon Hill put this book together not to make a million dollars, but to respond to the call and answer the question of what successful people had in common. And he took on that quest. He took on the challenge and it took him twenty-five years to fulfil it. Now, I imagine it was wonderful interviewing these amazing humans who have achieved so much and Hill's perspective is insightful but he could never have foreseen the book's success or that it would touch millions of lives and continue to have an impact for decades to come. *Think and Grow Rich* is now a movie and there is also a magazine in which I recently shared my own story.

I encourage you to read this book. It will give you a foundation for success that you could never have imagined. And think of the power of what you can achieve if you really put love into what you are pursuing. We plant seeds of intention and then we nurture the opportunities and follow up on the inspired thoughts that come when those seeds are planted. We nurture them to flourish with love.

It reminds me of an experiment conducted with two batches of seeds. One batch was nurtured, given water, light, whatever they needed scientifically to grow. The other batch also had their basic requirements met but with the addition of being talked to and having a lot of loving energy directed to them. The seeds that were nurtured with loving energy grew bigger, brighter, healthier than the seeds that were supplied with only their basic needs.

Think about that for a moment. Think of the power of that energy. Why would you choose to put any other energy into what you are growing? Think about your children. If you don't have children, think about when you were a child. I know whenever I think about my children, I feel so much love for them. They know they're loved unconditionally. Why? I know the value of unconditional love because I was gifted it as a child and it was only as I grew up that I realised not everyone experienced this.

That foundation of knowing that you're unconditionally loved is the greatest gift of all, no matter a family's wealth. As children, we had everything we needed but not a lot of extras. I did have that unconditional love and that is a gift. The greatest gift of all is love and it helped me to grow into the person I am today.

And I want to give and I want to share my love with everyone because love is infinite. We cannot run out of it. The more that we give, the more we have to give. Living with an open heart requires courage. You need to know yourself better than anyone else knows you so that you can stand true to yourself and not get caught up with negativity.

Sometimes in being true to yourself and being loving those people who are not ready to receive that will not react as you hope. But that's not about you. That's them. When you're on the success tangent, surround yourself with your people, the people who love to receive what you give and love to raise you up. That is love. That is success.

We're always on a quest for success because we're ever evolving, and when we achieve one thing we roll onto a new cycle and we're at the beginning of something new again. So we're forever progressing and love is sharing that. We are here to share what we learn with others. I have people who say to me, "Are you are you crazy? Why do you show people how to publish their own books?"

Why would I keep that to myself? If somebody is willing to put in the work that I put in, then they deserve the results that I get. If everyone finds their way there's no competition. When we show up and share and help someone on their journey to make it easier for them, that is something wonderful and that has to be celebrated. That is love, sharing and caring. It's not only the one person who receives it. Everyone around them benefits and the ripples of one absolute definite act of love are widespread. That is why we need to be open to receiving. It took me a while to learn that I was always the giver.

I like to give. It makes me feel good so I receive in that way. But I also understand that I have to be able to receive from others who choose to gift me. There's nothing wrong with that. It's beautiful.

Only you know your personal definition of success, whether it is in business, love, lifestyle. For me, success is having this beautiful balance between family and ambition.

I'm an ambitious person. I like to achieve things. It makes me feel good. I like to help people and financial stability is part of that because if I'm earning well, then I'm able to do more. That's what money is for, to keep things going, not for hoarding away.

It's for keeping the wheels in motion, because as we need it, the money will come to make those things happen. There is success in loving my children, loving myself, loving where I am in life, loving what I do, just loving my life. Yet my life could be someone else's nightmare.

I'm not joking. I'm a mom of six. I live in a little house not far from the beach. It's beautiful here in Perth, Australia. I feel so grateful. But you can look at the other side of it. There's never a moment where it's not busy. There's always something to do. But I was gifted a beautiful gift from my mother and I'm able to switch off in between things so that my mind can be calm when needed.

I live on the other side of the world from my family and I miss them. I don't focus on that because now is not the time for me to put energy into them because I can't take action on that. What I can take action on is my beautiful life that I have created by design for myself and my family. And each member of my family may choose to design their life differently, but they will feel supported on that. For me being a successful parent is guiding my children, not controlling them. And each of them is different. Yes, it takes more effort on my part, but to watch them grow up into beautiful individuals, for me that is success.

Everyone has different priorities in their success quest so understand what that is for you. When you understand what success means to you, that is in itself success. Enjoy.

Surround yourself with those who you choose to be with.

LOVE AND RELATIONSHIPS

I have always been a difficult person to be in a relationship with and not because I'm unlovable. In fact, the love that I give is so pure, so, so pure that it really connects with those I gift it to and it's absolutely genuine. The reason I'm hard to be with is that I don't need somebody else's love to be validated. I already love myself and I know that is enough.

When I choose to receive love, it's powerful. When our love comes together, it is a powerful energy that when projected into something united is mind blowing and effective. I don't say this lightly. It's from experience. I'm a total romantic and the dynamics of love when two people come together, the energy exchange, the connection, you don't question that when it's true love.

You may pinch yourself and wonder, "Oh, my goodness, is this happening" but when you embrace it, don't overthink it and simply bask in the essence of it, that is the most beautiful thing ever. Of course, as humans we overcomplicate things and destroy things and self-sabotage. And that's tragic. But when we show up in love and connect in love and that's reciprocated, that is special and should never be questioned, judged, or sabotaged in any way.

When two loving energies combine, they create life and that's a miracle. When my first child was delivered into the world, I felt like my heart could burst with love. As a mum of six, I thought, "Oh my goodness, am I going to have enough love to give?"

Absolutely. You know, I have enough love to give the whole globe if they're receptive of it. There's nothing like a hug. I love hugging my children. I get so much out of it when our hearts connect. It's a physical feeling and one that the kids need. My fifteen-year-old still comes to me for a hug. And it's not just a quick hug, it's an actual hug filled with love that pours into them because they need it, because being a teenager is tough when you are getting to know who you are.

Love needs to be reciprocated, to be given equally on both sides for it to be this beautiful harmony that creates more beautiful things in our world. But it's OK for you to stand in love for yourself and know yourself and know that you are love, that you have that to give their confidence.

Some people may feel inadequate, they may feel things about that, and that's so sad.

When we all truly take time to stand in our own love

within ourselves and love ourselves first, everyone benefits because then we set a precedent on how we deserve to be loved. Sparks fly when two people get together and they make love. Is that not the most beautiful, sensual thing that you can ever give to someone?

It's like an aphrodisiac. It's like a drug, an absolute euphoria. Exploration of each other's bodies comes into play because you can trust each other, and the most beautiful connection happens because of that love.

When it stands the test of time there's nothing more beautiful than a couple in their eighties or nineties looking at each other adoringly because they know they're loved, they love each other. You can be guaranteed they have had a lifetime of ups and downs and maybe were on the brink of divorce at times, but they've come through it and they are there together at the end of their lifetime, still loving each other, accepting and honouring that love.

Love needs to start with yourself, really knowing and loving yourself and allowing that love to flow through you first and then pour into others.

Take a moment to stop and look at your relationship with yourself. Do you love yourself? Flaws and all? My goodness, I am not perfect. No way. But I know what I want and how to get it. I know how to give and how to have that balance between giving and receiving. I know how to love and I know how to pour back into myself when I need to.

I know the value of keeping my cup full so that I can pour love into others. Don't sacrifice too much of yourself so that you are left depleted because that is of no use to anybody. As I write this, I am sitting in bed snuggled up because I have a head cold. I don't want it to last long so I've taken to my bed to work. Already I feel better because I'm talking about love and love is all healing.

    So think about your relationship with yourself and others and how you want those relationships to be and pour love into that. See what happens, what flourishes.

*Lead with your heart, do the
right things for the right reason,
and choose love every chance you get.*

KIM OAKHILL

LOVING ENERGY AS YOUR SUPER FUEL

Numerous times a day, I use loving energy as a super fuel. Of course, I need to ensure that I have a never-ending supply to use and that is where the self-love chapter comes in handy. When you harness this energy to achieve your desires or help someone, something beautiful happens.

When I set an intention, I will also inject some loving energy in there to get it started and when inspired thoughts and opportunities aligned with that intention present themselves to me I have the courage to say yes to the YES's and NO to the definite no's and the distracting maybe's.

Choosing love is a choice, you can equally choose hate, but I hope that after reading this book you won't. From my experience of making amazing things happen in my life I will always choose love. Not only do I get more satisfying results I also get to live through a higher vibration which is turn gifts me happiness

Most of us strive for happiness but seek it externally when in fact happiness comes from within. No external source should be in control of your happiness. The gatekeeper of your happiness must be you because your internal navigation system works one hundred per cent in your favour, not only to benefit you but also everyone around you. When someone bestows the control of their happiness on us, or we do the same to someone else it is an unfair expectation because they don't beat through your heart.

Connecting to love in order to achieve your heart's desire, whatever that may be, is something you can all do instantly when you learn how.

When you choose to react through love every time it has an impact beyond any thought capacity we have, it ripples further and wider than we could ever know. But we actually don't need to know in order to receive the benefits in our life. All you need to know is that when you choose to react with love only good things come from that.

My tips for harnessing love as a super fuel are:

1. Learn how to react with love; make love a habit.
2. Be open to all goodness that comes your way.
3. Accept energetic and physical gifts with huge gratitude.
4. Accept compliments with gratitude.
5. When unsure of what to do, think "what would love do?"
6. Understand that you don't need to understand. Love is not a thinking process, it is an open-hearted process.

One of the key things to note about loving energy is that there is an unlimited supply. Love multiplies the more we use it. It is miraculous like that. I never try to understand that, I just allow myself to know it.

When you live choosing love, if you stumble in life you never fall so far that you can't dust yourself off and get back on track.

*Pursue an income stream
doing what you love.*

A LOVE FUELLED EXPERIENCE

I want to share with you a love fuelled experience I had recently. I'm usually the person who creates the events, hosts people there and creates the experience. This time the call was loud for me to go and bask in the energy and experience of an Ausmumpreneur retreat with the amazing Katy Gardner and Peace Mitchell. I was going to relax, recharge and rejuvenate my energy because I was at capacity.

I know myself well enough to know when I need to stop. A big thing for me is leaving my family, and I don't like to be away from them too long but I knew that to be my best self, I needed to go away and recalibrate. I just knew I had to go so

I set the intention. My husband knows whenever something calls me like this there's no point trying to talk me out of it. He went along with it even though flying to the other side of Australia in the middle of a pandemic wasn't ideal. Any number of scenarios could happen including finding myself in a fourteen-day lockdown and unable to return home, all for the sake of three nights to recharge and recalibrate.

I could have gone to a local hotel in Perth and written my heart out for three days or simply recharged. But that wasn't the way it was supposed to happen. I needed to go and experience this retreat for the divinity that was to come with it. A lot of serendipitous things came into play, a lot of unexpected alignments. I was adamant that I wanted to get a direct flight from Western Australia to Queensland, even though that meant I would arrive thirty-six hours before the retreat.

Now, a significant number for me is 22. I think of it as 'my' number. My house is number 22 in our street. Exciting things often happen for me connected with 22 and I know big things are going to happen this year especially as we move into 2022 with the alignment of numbers. What I didn't realise until I arrived there was that the retreat was being held on the twenty-second week of the year. I just knew I had to be there.

Luckily I listened to my knowing because I went over and Katy picked me up and I spent a day with these two amazing women followed by a night on my own, the first time I had been alone in a house in more than twenty years.

Wow. There I was in a beautiful little beachside bungalow beside Mission Beach, Queensland, which is the energy porthole of Australia. I hadn't known that. Then during the retreat there was a full moon lunar eclipse. Twenty women came together and this divine thing was happening in the energy porthole of Australia. Holy moly.

It was such a life changing experience. From the moment I was picked up to the moment I left, every single thing Katy and Peace did was with loving intention. Everything was fuelled through love, down to the minutest details such as how things would be positioned to exclusive cutlery in each bungalow.

Every single detail was put together with so much loving intention. Every experience we had was felt through that love and not one thing went wrong. It was flawless. Obviously, behind the scenes of events things do go wrong, but everything flowed and was as it should have been.

Every experience was harnessed and embraced. I only went there to rejuvenate, hang out with amazing women and just recharge yet I had breakthroughs myself even though I felt that I was pretty much together. Of course, we're always a powerful work in motion, regardless of the goals we achieve. We're always evolving. We're always going through these cycles of evolution and that retreat marked the start of a new cycle for me, the merging of my business and my authorship.

I'm successful and I'm comfortable and confident in my authorship because I know that what I am sharing changes lives. It connects with and inspires people. But imagine that you've been working ten years in your employment. You're really confident, you've really built traction and brand awareness and lots of people want to work with you.

You have this presence. You show up authentically and confidently in that space alongside people. And then you're called to something else because you've got all of the publishing wrapped up, you've worked to bring it to a certain place and it's there. You're able to serve well, but you've now made room for magic. That's what was happening. The call to share, to start putting energy into my writing and to show authors what can happen when you do put yourself all in to your project.

I showed up at this retreat perceived by everyone as the publisher but I was really there as the author and the two merged because of the loving environment that was created for that merger to flourish. I experienced breakthroughs because I had the space and clarity to embrace them and also harvested the insight and knowledge that came through the other participants.

That was their gift to me because of the amazing energy and connection we had. It was super powerful. The two worlds of my authorship and my business collided and were embraced. Before I left spoke at a business conference attended by Queensland government representatives and heard later that one of the attendees considered my talk the highlight of the presentations.

The universe sends affirmations when you on the right path, signs to let you know to keep going. That was my signpost. But the ultimate thing was the love that fuelled that retreat. And I know how much energy it takes to put in that kind of loving intention that comes from the most authentic place.

Genuine, absolutely. Giving heart bliss. Yeah. So be mindful of the experiences you create. If you're creating events, harness and embrace all the love you can and inject that into the event. I promise you your event will stay with people much longer. Attending this retreat was such a deep, profound experience for me. I always inject love into my events and will now be injecting so much more because of the inspiration I gained and what I experienced.

So it has a ripple effect. Imagine if you have twenty or a hundred or a thousand people experiencing that love-fuelled event and each one of them taking something away from it and creating that experience for somebody else. That's the foundation for change. That's the foundation for love to ripple through our world.

That's when we feel at home and that we belong. That's when we feel loved and cherished. And that is what we all should be able to feel openly without any overthinking, without ever feeling awkward. That's the kind of genuine connection we should be promoting around this amazing world.

Can you identify a love-fuelled experience you have had recently?

*The universe provided when I served,
and that, for me is love.*

CLIONA O'HARA

BONUS CHAPTER: THE ANSWER IS LOVE
(WRITTEN IN 2009)

The answer is 'LOVE'.
   What is the question?
   What is the key to true happiness?
   We all strive to be happy. No matter what circles we revolve in, our main goal is happiness. Whether it is materialistic or ambitious our end goal is achieving something that makes us, as individuals, feel happy. Many people strive for perfection. But who is it that determines what perfection is? We all have

our own ideals of perfection and aim for that, and why? To make us HAPPY!

Now armed with this information that feeling love makes us happy, what are you going to do about it? How do you get enough love to make you happy? I am pleased to tell you that you don't need to go seeking it; you just need to unlock the vault to your own self-love. By loving ourselves we will discover true happiness that no amount of material possessions will ever give us. When we access this love we will discover there is a never-ending supply all for ourselves that we can share with others and it will never dry up. In fact the more we spread our love, the more that is created and the more that comes back to us.

I like to think of it as a snowball. By starting off with a little ball of love and giving it the opportunity to grow by rolling it along and nurturing it, we enable it to become a greater ball of love. Then in no time at all it will be ready to roll down the mountain of life gathering more and more love all of the time. What do we have at the end? A great BIG ball of Love that everyone can feel and enjoy. Did you know we can heal our body and mind just by loving ourselves? Simply by taking the time to listen to the signals your body is giving, you have the power within you to perform miraculous things.

> *"Love creates miracles, Love creates magic."*
> **Sascha Brooks**

According to author Louise L. Hay, by loving yourself and affirming this love through positive affirmations you can heal ANY ailment or illness you may have. Yes, it is that amazing!

Tips on how to love yourself

Self-love may sound easy to do, but it is a process that needs focus and time to blossom. People who have suffered childhood neglect and abuse will find it difficult to take the steps towards self-love. Here are some tips I came across to assist in overcoming these steps.

- Compile a list of things OTHERS like about you. Ask people who know and love you what they like about you. This is a first step towards realising your personal qualities. Write your own list of what YOU like about yourself. Be honest with yourself. If you are having trouble, think about the people you love and the qualities you admire in them. Do you have those same qualities?
- Create a feel-good notebook/box. Invest in a notebook or box that makes you feel good when you see it. Use it to keep these lists. Look at its contents every time you feel low or if you are made to feel low by someone else.
- Read these lists often. Make reading these wonderful things about you a regular occurrence in your life as often as you can. Every time you do, it will eliminate one time you felt bad or were made to feel bad and replace it with a positive.
- Add a note. Make yourself tune in to hearing the positives about yourself, no longer the negatives. Write each of them down and add them to your collection.

- You are your own best friend. We all love our friends but I have news for you: YOU are your own best friend. Love yourself as you do your friends. Close your eyes, feel the love you have for them and project it onto yourself. Store that feeling.
- Give yourself a break. Learn to be compassionate and forgiving to yourself. Would you be so hard and judgmental on your friends or loved ones? No, you would probably be there offering support. Feel that love and compassion for yourself.
- Love comes from within. A well of love exists within us all and we can access it whenever we choose. Access self-love regularly. You deserve to be loved, so love yourself.
- Affirmations. By using affirmations you are registering positives in your brain which will help you to feel good. Things like: I am an amazing, loving and caring person. I deserve the very best in my life. Pin them up in the areas you are in most often—your car, computer, fridge, at work. Feel them.
- Nurture yourself. Do things for yourself that make you feel loved and cared for. A nice pampering session, some meditation, a wonderful book, a peaceful walk. These are some things we can gift to ourselves that will enhance our loving potential.
- Listen. Take a quiet moment to listen to yourself and the signs you are receiving. It may take time to connect but by giving yourself some time each day to listen to your inner guide you will more easily recognise your needs and desires.

- Look. This will be a hard one for many. I know it was for me. Look in a mirror; look straight into your eyes and tell yourself "I love you". Do this every day as often as you feel comfortable and you will find it will get easier. I found it very emotional the first time I did it. For me the eyes are the gateway to the soul and I felt an intense feeling at that moment.

These are all tips you can use to assist on your journey to self-love. You need only select those you feel will work for you. It can be hard to give yourself this gift at first but always know that you have the courage and strength within you and you deserve it! The love you attract from others comes from you initially. If you don't love yourself then it is really hard for others to love you.

I know this because I went through a period where I did not take the time to love me. I was just motoring along, loving my family and doing what I thought was right. But it wasn't OK. My relationships were straining around me and I was not being fulfilled, my soul was perishing. Since learning to love myself, I radiate love and in every aspect of my life all of my relationships have blossomed too. I have so much love now within and I know that I will always glow.

When I talk about loving myself I don't mean being arrogant; this is when someone thinks only of themselves. No, self-love is when someone has a strong sense of respect for and confidence in themselves. This is usually taught in childhood through honesty, acceptance and unconditional love. However most parents have their own issues of self-doubt and limiting beliefs which they project onto their children consciously and unconsciously and so a cycle of self-rejection repeats itself.

So let's break the cycle and the stigma attached to self-love. In order to truly love another we need to first love ourselves. It is important not only for us but for our families and for humanity. Everything in life will be better now that we know 'The Answer'.

> *"Love is the great miracle cure. Loving ourselves works miracles in our lives."*
> **Louise L Hay**

Share what you discover with others.

GUEST CONTRIBUTORS

If you do not appreciate the little things, you cannot accept the big things. You cannot love until you love yourself.

LEANNE MURNER

Cliona O'Hara

Universal love means to me that we are all connected and we are all cut from the same cloth. And I believe that we are we are spiritual beings in a physical body. We **are** soul, we don't have a soul, and I believe we're all of the same family as spiritual beings. For me, universal love is that connection to my fellow man and woman and the other beings on this earth and we are here to serve one another.

I know we're here to serve. Each soul was sent to Earth with a purpose and tied to their purpose is their gifts and their talents unique to them. So the law of love for me is serving those gifts and talents to our fellow man and woman. I was in my mid- twenties when I realised this.

At the time I was at a very low part in my life and I was living in New York. I was really struggling financially, emotionally, in every way. I was bankrupt. And I remember crying out to the universe for help. I was literally on my knees crying and saying, "Help. This cannot be the way," and I remember, in my opinion, God telling me, "You have to go serve. You have to go serve." I remember saying to myself, "Well, how am I going to serve? I don't have anything to serve."

I started really tapping into my intuition and following that inner voice and that guidance. And even though I had no physical money and I had nothing really to offer, I thought, I just listened to my inner voice and I was guided to go do some charity work nearby in a local church. They had a soup kitchen and I said, "You know, I'll go there and I'll serve in the soup kitchen, that's serving."

They gave me a job in the office when they found out that I had computer skills so I volunteered for a couple of weeks and I was serving, I was following this inner voice. Yet every time I went home, I had no food. I ran out of food, I ran out of money, and I was an immigrant with no papers at the time in New York City so I would eat at the church, come home and then go back every day and serve. Within a couple of weeks I manifested three green checks and it was three tax returns of twenty seven thousand dollars in total.

The universe provided when I served, and that, for me is love. It's not about me for my personal benefit. It's about growing and creating and giving and serving while we're here.

As far as loving our neighbour and loving humanity, I believe we're here to serve. But we're also here to leave everyone we meet with the impression of an increase, which is, leave everybody better off, whether it's a kind word or helping them in some way, shape or form. We're here. We have to leave everybody with the impression of increase.

I have learnt to love myself entirely and accept myself the way that I was born and made, and I know that I'm perfectly made and I'm created in the image of God. And I am a creator. I'm a creative being because I am an extension of God. I'm a creator, so have completely surrendered to loving myself for that reason. If I'm a creator and I'm created in the image of God, then for me to love myself is to love God and vice versa.

I believe I'm perfectly made. I believe we're all perfectly made and we're here to love and we're here to serve and we're here to leave everybody better off.

Kim Oakhill

Intro

What do you get when you cross a boss lady, investor backed social enterprise founder, corporate lawyer with a woo woo moon worshipping, conscious uncoupled boho celebrant meditation lady? Me! You get me!

The biggest juxtaposition of a human you can get. I'm in love with love, and I embody everything that yin and yang is all about. Feminine and masculine. Soft, yet strong. And when I hear the words, "the Law of Love", I think of this balance, the yin and yang, the gentle and the fierce, and I am living proof that both of these elements can not only co-exist, but they are essential to living a beautiful, big, full, passionate life.

Leading from the heart (feminine/love), but using the knowledge, determination and power from the head (masculine/law) to birth our ideas and dreams out into our world.

I'm Kim Oakhill, and this is my story.

Bio

My bio says:

Kim Oakhill is a Mumma, funky modern celebrant, and heart-centred, award-winning entrepreneur from Port Stephens, NSW.

She has two children, a creative, musical little legend,

Conway (8) and a free- spirited, sassy fire cracker, Dusty Mae (6) and two bonus (step) kiddos, a sporty, caring little dude, James (9) and a little princess, crystal lover, Veronica (4). Following a few dark years navigating a painful divorce, she found the love of her life, her strong, masculine, Viking king, Michael.

Kim grew up on 25 acres on the Mid North Coast, and after Year 12, lived in Finland for 12 months on Rotary Youth Exchange. She told the Rotarians she wanted to go to the other side of the world for a cultural experience, so living in the Arctic Circle couldn't have been more on point!

After returning from Finland, she moved to Newcastle and completed her law degree by distance, while working full time in a law firm as a law clerk. About half way through her studies, she realised that law was not for her, (interestingly, she felt her "heart wasn't in it…") but continued her studies at night, swapping the suits for a super hero outfit, and spent her days brightening the lives of seriously ill children for the Starlight Children's Foundation. Once graduating with that piece of paper, she then ventured into the high-paced corporate world of commercial contracting and project management. [So much yin and yang in this paragraph!]

After becoming a mum, a passion was ignited within to create a legacy for her children to be proud of. She explored a new path of creative, soul fulfilling ventures and became a very successful modern marriage celebrant and meditation facilitator.

In February 2016, following the death of her friend's little girl, she founded Helpful Love; an award-winning social enterprise which offers practical domestic help in lieu of flowers during times of tragic loss.

Kim's mission is to grow the Helpful Love movement across

Australia and once established and blossoming beautifully, across the globe.

Kim says, "My purpose is to leave the world a better place than when I entered it, and to ensure no one ever crosses my path without feeling happier than when they met me."

Law of Love [Personal Perspective]

What my bio doesn't say, is that I have battled and straddled the two worlds—the love (the yin) and the law (the yang) to merge this beautiful tapestry together to create, my bio; my journey of life.

I have always been a high achiever. I guess to put a label on it, a type A personality. A perfectionist. Constantly striving to do better. To be better. To make my mark. And I've learned, through love, triumph, success, grief and loss, that when I surrender the control (the masculine or yang soul within my body) and lead from my heart, to do the right things for the right reasons, that is from a place of love. And love wins, always.

When I think of the Law of Love from a personal perspective, I am reminded of my darkest days. Navigating a painful, challenging, unwanted (at the time) experience; the ending of my marriage with my children's father. Divorce is something so truly legal. Something that was once all about love.

How does a type A personality, a perfectionist, tell the world she's failed?

By choosing love. I chose to tap into my yin, my soft, feminine, creative, spiritual inner goddess to surrender my control, to release the strong, forceful grip and to simply trust the process and the journey. The law of love.

There were many, many things I could have shared with the world about our separation. The lies, the betrayal, the deception, the sleepless nights... But I believed that until I healed the wound within, I would simply bleed all over others who didn't cause the pain through my projection onto them to listen to my story, to feel better inside. But that is not what I wanted for those in my world.

As difficult as it was at the time, I chose love. I chose to heal my wounds through meditation, mindfulness, positive affirmations, crystals, journaling and all the things that helped release the toxicity from my mind and soul out of my body and out of this consciousness.

After doing the work privately, this is what I shared with the world:

Love is unconditional. Relationships are not...

I love this wonderful man. On our wedding day, I promised to love and respect him for the beautiful soul that he is, and never try to change him.

I have changed. Massively. And I continue to grow, evolve, heal and expand to live my biggest, best, bright and sparkly life. My very best life, and be the very best me that I can be. [He] hasn't changed so much... he prefers a smaller, quieter, simple life. Neither is better nor worse—it just is what it is.

A few months ago, [He] and I realised that we were unable to be whole as individuals while we desperately tried so hard to be a partner to someone on a totally different playing field. It exhausted us, and saddened us deeply.

It broke our hearts but as we both loved and respected each other so so much (and still do), we made the heartbreaking decision to set each other free.

We have consciously uncoupled.

(Yes, the term made famous by Hollywood couples, but also

the most incredibly beautiful and peaceful way to separate a partnership).

We've done the conscious uncoupling program, and continue to do the individual work on ourselves.

To look at us from the outside (and even as a fly on the wall in our home), you probably wouldn't even know that we aren't a "couple" (except that [He] has a funky granny flat he's decking out down the back, and I have totally Kim-ified my bedroom with crystals, fairy lights, inspirational quotes, affirmations, sage sticks and even a beaded chandelier!)

We are proud of ourselves for doing our best to remain a couple for the last few years, but we've learnt that we are just two beautiful beings, on two very different paths. And we are the bestest of friends when the pressure of staying together "for better for worse" / "even if you make each other incredibly miserable" is removed.

Uncoupling/separation can bring up so much internal pain. Shame, guilt, embarrassment, judgement, jealousy—fear, so much fear! But I'm so grateful to be surrounded by so much love in my life, and to be learning and growing, and becoming stronger and more in tune with who I am and who I want to be as I go along. I'm also super grateful to [Him] for committing to work through his "stuff" too.

To sum it up—we're happier than ever! Our little people have two parents who are such better friends than partners, and we're at a place in our lives where we are simply honouring the present moment—without putting too much pressure, worry and angst about the "what ifs" of the future.

All we have is this moment, and while we acknowledge there are likely to be a few rough bumps along the way as we navigate this new reality, and working through emotions that pop up as triggers and fear hit us, we are committed to working through this as the very best versions of ourselves that we can be.

This is the law of love at work.

This is consciously choosing a beautiful path for ourselves, despite it being a dark and scary trail. It's easy to fall into the trap of the victim mode; to replay and relive the traumatic event over and over again. To tell the world of our pain, to use the legal system to our advantage and to spread misery to all who will listen to stop us from feeling so very alone.

We have a choice. We can choose darkness, or we can heal and push through to the light.

The yin supported me to sit with my feelings, to process, heal and move forward. The yang helped me to navigate the legal aspects of an uncoupling. To be fierce and assertive when I needed to be, but respectful, reasonable and fair. I loved the quote "Getting divorced sucks. Being divorced doesn't".

At times, I needed to be strong, and to back myself. Sometimes, that meant choosing love for myself. Both elements needed to dance simultaneously; yin and yang, soft and strong, love and law. And I made it through—we all did.

Law of Love [Career Perspective]

When I think of the Law of Love from a career perspective, I am reminded of Jacinda Ardern's quote— "One of the criticisms I've faced over the years is that I'm not aggressive enough or assertive enough, or maybe somehow, because I'm empathetic, I'm weak. I totally rebel against that. I refuse to believe that you cannot be both compassionate and strong".

This is a classic example of the Law of Love at work!

A beautiful, strong leader, doing the right things for the

right reasons, heart-centred but ballsy enough to take on big egos for a greater purpose.

When pitching for investment for my social enterprise, Helpful Love, I encountered big egos, avaricious corporates and venture capitalists who were all about making money and trashing my business model. Helpful Love was born from love, grief and heartache, and while I was open to ideas to make a bigger impact, I was closed to the idea of taking money from grieving families' pockets to profit greedy shareholders. The law of love governs Helpful Love's existence, and as long as I am the gatekeeper and steward of this beautiful mission and vision, it will continue to be run from the heart, and not from the greedy hands of money grabbing protagonists.

To me, money is energy. It comes and it goes. So long as Helpful Love is helping those who need it, its existence is on purpose and doing exactly what it needs to do.

I remember being told by a mentor— "Helpful Love can't just run on love. You need to hustle! You need investment! You need marketing! You need profit at X% etc etc"

Well, I'm living proof that it actually can run on love. Love is energy, love is its own form of currency. With love as the driving force behind everything I do, I am unstoppable. I'm a dreamer, and I'm a doer. And I use love to make my wildest dreams come true.

I also find that when I pursue a path from a place of love, the journey is effortless. It's a path of "ease and grace". When I'm leading from the heart, everything unfolds perfectly as it is meant to. Opportunities are presented to me, money flows, media and PR reps reach out to me, promotions fall in my lap… yet when I'm hustling for the wrong reason, for example, for an ego boost or for attainment instead of heartfelt desire, the process is harder. It's like there is a block or a greater force guiding me that I'm not quite following my path.

My corporate world is a heavily dominated masculine industry and workplace. There is an assumption that some females are there to simply fill the diversity quota. This is one of the reasons I love working there so much, and probably why I have tried to leave the corporate world several times in my career, but always feel the pull to stay right there.

Because I challenge this belief. I take pride in modelling heart-centred leadership in an industry that is dominated by masculine energy. And I'm good at it! And so are many others I have the privilege of working with.

Some of the greatest leaders I know (of all genders) demonstrate empathy and compassion. They genuinely care about people and they spend time investing in relationships. This is again, the law of love at work.

Dwight D Eisenhower quoted that "Leadership is the art of getting someone else to do something you want done because he wants to do it."

I take this one step further.

In my experience, if you treat people with genuine care and respect, get to know them, share the vision and take them on the journey with you, then this is heart-centred leadership. This is when your people will genuinely and enthusiastically jump on board.

If you don't win their hearts, they may still do something for you because you have commanded it. But they won't do it because they want to. They'll do it because they have to. And eventually, they'll probably leave because they won't feel valued, appreciated or empowered. They won't feel the love.

As humans, we all have a deep, intense desire to be loved.

There is a wealth of research on this including Bowlby's evolutionary theory of attachment. This theory suggests that we come into the world biologically pre-programmed to form attachments with others, because this helps us to survive.

So, if we are born into this world to form attachments to survive, then we must consider the perception that our modern world is governed by legislative laws, governments, powerful people in high places, money, oil, gold…

I'd argue that it's *actually* governed by love and a desire for human connection.

Final thoughts

During my counselling sessions with my psychotherapist, I clearly remember saying, "I'm just so angry. I can't get past it. I have so much anger." My therapist said, "Do you know what emotion sits under anger? Sadness. It's OK to be sad."

I cried and cried and cried…

After that, I did some EMDR (Eye Movement Desensitisation and Reprocessing) therapy with her. I then sat with my feelings and said, "I'm so incredibly sad. It's sad, isn't it? It's all over and I'm just so, so sad." My therapist said, "And do you know which emotion sits under sadness? Love."

And with that revelation, I was able to heal.

The Law of Love is so truly powerful. Love is a balance of yin and yang. It can be debilitating or exhilarating—bringing us to our knees or launching us to unleashing our wildest dreams.

Lead with your heart, do the right things for the right reason, and choose love every chance you get.
Kim Oakhill

Websites:

- Small Business Owner:
  www.kimoakhill.com
- Small Business Owner:
  https://www.thebreathingspaceportstephens.com/
- CEO and Founder:
  www.helpfullove.com

Social Media:

- LinkedIn:
  www.linkedin.com/in/kimoakhill
- Facebook:
  www.facebook.com/helpfullove.com.au
- Facebook:
  www.facebook.com/KimOakhillModernCivilCelebrant

Taryn Claire Le Nu

I once had Cancer for two weeks.

At the end of 2016, I was diagnosed with Invasive Lobuloma Carcinoma (breast cancer) which had spread to my lymph nodes. I soon discovered that most people met me from their own place of fear, impacting me adversely. I could do fear all by myself and I didn't need more fear, I needed the love frequency to help me raise my own vibration.

Fear has an inaudible infrasound of 19 hertz. It's the same inaudible frequency that they pump through a horror movie, leaving you sitting on the edge of your seat, absolutely terrified even when no other sound is emanating from the screen. If you press mute, that sense of dread rapidly dissipates. I needed friends and family to not just press mute, I needed them to switch to a different channel.

From the moment I was diagnosed it triggered a series of Radical Acts of Self-Love. At the top of my list was setting Boundaries with an impressive capital B. I put myself in charge of teaching people about the way they inadvertently and unconsciously presented their fear to me.

Most folks are ill-equipped with the perfect response when met with someone else's grief or trauma, their words fail them, with their unconscious fear lurking in the wings ultimately betraying them.

My mantra became, "If you don't know what to say, if

you've never been in this position before (and you don't want to upset me or add to my fear), could you rather send me a simple love heart? What I really need from you in this very moment is love. I have a far greater use of Love than of Fear".

By gently guiding people to send me love instead of fear, I upgraded my own experience into a more loving space ripe for healing. By using the energy of their love to raise my vibration, to meet cancer from a place of love not fear was empowering.

Love has a frequency of 528 hertz, super charged with the capacity to heal.

I found that people were grateful to be led and guided in how to respond and I soon became overwhelmingly swamped with SO much love! It was incredible. I got sent all sorts of love hearts in varying shapes and forms that people found and photographed on their walks on the beach, clouds in the sky, leaves on trees and the froth on coffee. As my friends and family felt more confident with how to handle me, so their capacity for showing intentional love grew. Each time I received a love heart, I would close my eyes and visually breathe that love heart in, absorbing the energy and the intended vibration into my entire being. It felt unbelievably good. It was powerful and supported me to lock in the vibration for healing into every cell in my body through the power of love.

Love is the capacity to heal and love is the capacity to empower.

When we give love, we are creating a magnetic unseen charge and sending that out into the ethers. Showing love is creating a vibration and a frequency that activates the law of attraction where like attracts like. We may however, receive the love back from a completely different direction to where we originally sent our love. While I'd spent years cultivating love at the forefront of my practice, nourishing and nurturing people; with my diagnosis, I got showered with love from complete and utter strangers to the power of ten. It came as a beautiful, unexpected surprise. People who had never been a recipient of my love were showing up to give me their love. It was humbling and an eye-opening experience of living through the Law of Love in motion.

People I didn't know sent me Camilla scarves and kaftans, gifts, cards and flowers. Strangers sent beautiful messages of support and love hearts every day via social media. It was so unexpected. None of these people owed me their love and yet they gave it so freely. This holds enormous power to heal.

Years ago I watched an incredible interview where Oprah was interviewing Jill Bolte Taylor, a neuroanatomist who had had a stroke. She studied the way the brain worked, and next minute she actually experienced having a stroke for herself. She discovered that when you've had a stroke, you're not so much in the physical world. She could sense and feel the doctor's mood as he was walking down the corridor before he even entered her room. She knew what his state of mind was because she was now using something outside of her physical form to process it. Her insights were profound: people need to take personal responsibility for the energy they bring to your space.

> *"We have the power to choose who and how we want to be in the world each and every moment, regardless of what external circumstances we find ourselves in."*
> *Dr Jill Bolte Taylor*

What I know for sure is that when you bring the energy of LOVE to a space, you can't go wrong! As I prepare to celebrate my 5-year Thriver&Survivor milestone, I know that LOVE has played a huge role in where I am today.

Taryn Claire Le Nu
WEBSITE: www.tarynclairelenu.com
SOCIALS:
fb: Taryn Claire Le Nu
insta: @tarynclairelenu

Patricia Lovell

I asked myself and the Angels that walk with me a question: *What words do I use to describe what love is for me right now in this moment and how can I share that with another? What comments can I make? Where do I start to speak about Love as an energy?* I was stuck then the words began to flow and it seems as though they are not only for me.

We forget the simplicity of Love. We complicate it and think that we must feel it dramatically in forceful waves. We may experience that in regard to romantic love or in friendship.

Love as energy creates warmth and we can open our hearts to receive it through our breath. When our hearts feel full and warm, we can then spread it throughout all the cells of our physical body. Then to our mental and emotional bodies and beyond. Connected to all that is.

Experiencing the joy and simplicity of that connection and our soul's intention to know and be love.

Love is and always will be our birthright. We may feel its absence when we choose fear or anger and frustration.

We leave love. Love never leaves us. We simply tune back into it as it's like a musical score or theme that is always playing in the background of our daily lives. We control the volume. We may tune in more bass or treble to a harmony that suits us individually.

As I write these words, I feel the healing power of love which unites us all.

Love liberates us. It expands, never contracts and never judges. It is our choice to embrace and expand or dismiss it and contract. A choice that will create joyful lives where challenges can be overcome or one in which the struggles cast us in a victim role.

Regardless there is no judgement.

Love is and always will be who we are.

This is where I sit now with Love.

And it is as though I am on a mountain top. One that is more plateau these days. The air and sky are clear and filled with sparkling sunshine. I have a clear view as I look ahead and as I look behind me, I can see the mountains and the valleys that I descended into and climbed out of to bring me to this place. The highs and the lows. I can acknowledge that who I am now has been forged through love, even though it may not have seemed so at the time.

From the vantage point of this awareness, I can see love in my struggles to grow and climb out of the valleys. I have a true understanding of the words of Marianne Williamson: "Love brings up everything unlike itself." My life has been my own journey to experience the energy of love so of course all that wasn't love was going to be reflected to me and experienced. Not to hurt me but to clear my path to this plateau.

Looking back, I can see the personal and spiritual revolution that was required and which took place. A revolution, not to replace but to reveal my original pure, Love essence. A revolution to change long held beliefs about what love was or wasn't. Or about my worthiness to be loved or that love needed to be earned. I can see my struggles to bring light to my darkness where my beliefs, blockages and wounds were stuck. I understand now that the beliefs and rules I lived by had nothing to do with truth and were a barrier to accepting that Love is who I have always been.

I can now embody the awareness that we are larger than life souls arriving on Mother Earth struggling to fit into a little body, then forgetting our own magnificence in order to embark on the journey of remembering and awakening to Love. To become better versions of ourselves for ourselves and for the benefit of others and Mother Earth as well.

The first stirrings of my revolution to evolve started in the 1980s. I started to pay attention to myself. Noticing how I couldn't accept a compliment without it passing through my mind, *if only they knew me, they wouldn't say that*. Then noticing how easily I could dismiss my needs and keep giving love to others but not to myself. If I practised saying the words, I *love who* I *am* to myself, all the reasons why I couldn't do so would surface.

Deciding to set a course towards self-love was a painful process of letting go.

To evolve required the letting go of my attachments to those beliefs and rules I lived by and had taken more than thirty years to create and become entrenched.

My earth journey began in January 1951 and as I contemplate this it seems like time has passed in the blink of an eye.

My parents were among what is now referred to as the post-war battlers. I was the youngest of three children, my sister four years older, my brother in the middle.

These were also the times of fire and brimstone within the Catholic Church. As proud practising Catholics my parents held the belief that the priests and nuns were the chosen ones. Even when I spoke up about the vicious actions of some nuns, my concerns were met with, "Sister knows best". These were the times when sin and the Devil could take hold of you at any time.

Occasionally as that young child I could look past all the rules and regulations to what appeared to be a magical, starry sky and I was filled with wonder by an energy which would flow through me. This wonder connected me to a Jesus, (whom I now call Jeshua) of love and non-judgement. Unfortunately, I would only catch glimpses and have a small taste of this energy.

But the belief that love had to be earned and deserved became well entrenched.

I held the image of a God who kept a black book in which was written my every misdemeanour, unkind or selfish thought. Therefore, I created the rule that I had to be good and nice at all times.

I also took on the role as the family peacemaker. My father was an alcoholic and I saw it as my responsibility to keep everyone happy. Soothing the waves when my father's drinking caused disturbance distracted me from taking on the blame and shame for his drinking. I hadn't been good enough.

Being the peacemaker and keeping everyone happy came at a cost, it became a lonely place. And I was even less worthy of being loved if all my best efforts didn't work. It became automatic to suppress hurt, anger, resentment, even pain when trust placed in a sibling or friend was betrayed. Not only did love seem a long way away, but self-confidence was being chipped away to be replaced by self-doubt. But in spite of this I did genuinely care about others.

I look back on my child's struggles and without knowing it little me was always striving to be a better version of herself.

It was never thought of or suggested that we would all get along better and the world would be a better place if we loved ourselves first.

As the years rolled by the lack of confidence and self-doubt would keep me searching for love externally. If only someone would validate how responsible and caring I was I could love me. I now understand that external Love comes with conditions.

This search for love led me to being married and becoming a mother at the young age of eighteen. There's many a similar story to come out of 1969. Being pregnant meant being married. No more nursing career. For many years my good girl self would carry the guilt of it.

As more years roll by, I am the mother of three sons and they are never in doubt that I love them or feel that they need to earn my love. My husband succumbed to his addictive tendencies, becoming an alcoholic. Like my father, that didn't make him a bad man.

But once again I put myself back in that lonely place of feeling responsible. It was somehow my fault that he drank. Keeping the peace once again came at a cost.

The twists and turns of life were offering me other opportunities. I didn't have a name for it then but unknowingly I was teaching others what I most needed to learn.

For many years I was a volunteer Scripture teacher which led me to developing interfaith programs. While I wasn't filled with self-love I could teach and talk about a loving non-judgemental God. Working with intellectually and physically challenged children as an Integrative Aide I had them focus on

I can rather than *I can't*, each of them creating their own *I can* trees that they could keep adding branches to.

Love was sending me everything I needed to grow and arrive at that place of self-love. Love as a constant flow of energy from the Creator can often feel like a great mystery and denial of self-love an even greater mystery. Removing the blocks to self-love is painful as is any new birth. As well it was hard to grasp why I chose to experience everything that was unlike my real self.

Love has no opposites, the alternatives to love I was experiencing through fear, blame, shame and worthlessness were all of my choosing. Opening to Love brought loving people, programs and courses into my life, all opportunities to heal what my light in the darkness was revealing.

One loving person came in the form of Sister Colleen, as far removed from Catholic religious dogma as one could get. She trained me in various forms of spiritual and meditation practices. I was among a small group of people she introduced *A Course in Miracles* to; a course which turned me inside out and upside down and introduced me to the concept of there being only two emotions, Love and Fear.

The realisation grew within me that miracles occurred every time I chose to trust my own instincts rather than doubt them. A miracle occurred every time I made decisions based in love and not out of fear. In fact, I was learning that every negative thought I had ever had about myself could be transformed by love. Love on the inside not on the outside.

Miracles guided me into my training as a remedial therapist. I discovered that I had the ability to communicate with muscles and listen to their stories. Love seemed to pour through me. I was overwhelmed by the trust that clients displayed when they placed themselves in my hands. More than thirty plus years later I still have that sense of awe and privilege to be of service in whatever modality I use. My work is very grounding for me personally as I experience, after connecting with Source energy the healing power of Love flowing through me to each client.

During this revolution, after twenty years of marriage my husband and I divorced. When I think of that time, I simply consider that I was a flower growing in the wrong garden. Yes, it was an extremely painful time. Remember I was not only a good girl, but worked hard at being a good wife and mother. A common saying around that time was the fastest way through is to feel your feelings. And I began to feel them. It was a painful time of becoming and accepting me.

Love was at work as my first husband and I were able to continue as loving parents to our sons and together were able to jointly attend all family gatherings. I look back and acknowledge that I not only retained my ex-husband's surname for business purposes but because Lovell suited me because of my desire to Love all.

Miracles also led me to my Voice Dialogue training based on Jung's psychology of selves, which led to my understanding of how at a very young age I chose to be a pleaser and responsible in my family of origin in order to earn points and get love returned. Once this understanding dawned it really didn't make much sense that in my thirties and forties I was still living by my child's rules. Especially when it didn't work that well. Awareness then taught me to bring all aspects of my being into the light; the parts I like and the parts I dislike, out of the shadows. Sending love to every aspect, especially to my underdeveloped selves that needed nurturing, including self-love and confidence, then dancing with all these selves in the light.

Coming back into present time, here I am still on the plateau, sending Love behind along my timeline and ahead of me. I am happy to say my life is still a work of art in progress, because continuing to define and redefine myself hasn't stopped because I have reached a certain age. That thought may inspire joy or dread.

But I have learnt that rather than making someone or something else the Love of my life. I am the Love of my life. Then as naturally as night follows day, Love in the form of someone or something else will be in my life.

As a recovered Catholic and Pleaser, I please and take responsibility for myself first. I fill my inner well with Love and give from the spill over. When I live from a full well of self-love it's a natural progression to be kind and loving to others and in situations in a very genuine way with no expectation of what you may get in return.

Miracles continue to happen every day and in every moment when I choose Love. But choosing Love doesn't make the daily challenges of life go away, they still occur. I have learnt not to ignore any feeling, hurt or emotional pain. Difficulties in relationships still happen. Not going into denial is a form of love.

I try to resolve from that place within me that is love, not from fear as I honour each feeling.

I am grateful if another layer of an old pattern of behaviour has been revealed in my reaction to another or a situation. I allow myself to feel, for instance if it's self-doubt or a need to take control I acknowledge the feeling or desire then send it on its way with love. Set it free.

If there is a situation I cannot change or resolve, especially relationship upsets, I always ask the Angels of Love for help and place it in their hands. I am always in awe when through this letting go loving and peaceful solutions always arrive.

I use many tools including the Violet Flame of transmutation and self-forgiveness.

I forgive myself for ever having needed to have the experience, whatever it may have been. That act of forgiveness releases me and any others involved from judgement.

Any challenge that takes me into the valley, I can now run back up the mountain when powered by self-Love.

From that mountain top I see and know that living Love in action helps me attract into my life that which creates joy and the ability to discern what would detract from that joy. Living Love in action guides me towards activities and others whose energy I resonate with and away from that which would drain me. Which is not to say something is right or wrong, simply what helps me be the best version of myself.

Love in action is accepting that if I am love so is everyone regardless of their behaviour.

Love will always be Love and in all ways, I am Love. We are all Love whether it appears to be so or not. If we remember it or not, we are all part of the Creator's river of Light and Love.

Tomorrow once again on awakening I will set my daily intention that Love flows through my words, thought, actions and touch. Then see Love spreading out throughout the world to all living things then deep into Mother Earth.

Thank you, it is done. So be it.

Leanne Murner

How shifting from a negative to a loving outcome changed my life in one year.

I do not remember much of my childhood but what I do remember is that I felt everything was based around negativity. I had two parents that hated each other, one who worked days and the other working nights so they did not have to spend too much time together. Don't get me wrong, we never went without, it was just missing one thing, love.

My happy place as a child was out the back in a little shed where I would go and make timber clocks and decorate them with bark and gumnuts from nature to sell at a local handmade market. I loved being creative and when attending markets where I sold my products, I would receive so much positive feedback from all the customers. It was a great feeling being appreciated for what I was making. I would go home and share to my family how great a day I had had, only to be told, "People only bought your stuff because they felt sorry for you." It was clear that jealousy of me achieving something or having happiness was affecting this individual. I found it hard speaking about any achievements I had made throughout my life knowing I was not going to receive any encouragement or appreciation. I feel this had a massive impact on my life.

Moving into adulthood I struggled in relationships. I would get bored so quickly, I was not getting any joy or fulfilment, I had such a sense of loneliness, I felt I was just being used. I was searching for more; I then met my husband at work and it was love at first sight. I felt a sense of belonging with him and we were inseparable. I had all this love and affection I was not used to but it just felt right! I felt I had been walking a path to nowhere in survival mode and this path was an exciting new journey for me.

I have such an amazing bond and friendship with him and I would not be who I am today if he were not in my life. After thirteen amazing years I still get those belly butterflies when he sends me a cute little message to tell me how he would be lost without me. I feel such a sense of grounding now.

Whether we like to believe it or not we are carbon copies of our parents, good, bad or otherwise. It was not till we started to have children that I realised my comments and thought patterns were those of my parents, negative, controlling, and hateful at times. Never in a million years did I think I would become my parents. I struggled to be affectionate or show any compassion towards my children. I always dreamed of having my own family, but this was not how I wanted it to be.

I have an amazing relationship with my hubby, I have always discussed everything with him. I found out we both came from the same upbringing of negativity with parents hating each other, although he had received love and affection. We both made the conscious decision to change our life and not have it reflect the negativity of our childhood. I realised this meant an overhaul of ourselves and our thought processes, turning all that negative energy into creating a positive, loving life for our kids.

After having no affection as a child, as a parent I really struggled with showing affection and being a nurturing mother to my boys. It took a lot of hard work to change the mindset of "who I was" to "who I wanted to become". I was not handed a handbook for parenting; I did not want to raise my children in the same headspace I had experienced as a child.

I had had a dark cloud of negativity over me for years and it started to affect my working life. Any positive opportunity that came before me would soon disappear in a sea of doubts with "I am not good enough" or "I will not achieve anything" which started to flood my mind. Even those belly butterflies of excitement that appeared I would confuse with nervousness and convince myself "this is not for you; it's just nerves not excitement".

I wanted to stay in the "comfort zone" as many refer to it. This seemed to be where I was heading. I was taking one step forward and two back all the time. I feared being rejected or having that bubble burst. The constant putdown from my childhood was affecting me as an adult and restricting me moving forward to have dreams let alone fulfil them.

After my first business was well and truly flying along, I thought I had it made. Little did I know how wrong I was. I was focusing on supplying to the "little guy", smaller more consistent orders where the client could purchase less rather than in bulk. I found myself holding back once again. I did not want to get too big, scared of where I would end up, and found myself playing it safe.

At first it was my passion to give our clients what they wanted, but then with that negativity always in the shadows of my mind which led to me hating what I was doing, I was not being valued for the work I was doing. I had lost all the love and passion that I had for my business. I was searching for something to fuel that unhappy void I was experiencing. I struggled getting motivated and needed to follow my heart and do what I loved but I did not know what that was anymore.

I was nominated for an award for my business and had an opportunity to attend an awards conference but it took a lot of encouragement from my husband to attend. As the old saying goes, I came, I saw, I conquered. I didn't win anything, but I walked away a different person. I was so inspired by all the supportive women at this event, generally interested in what I was doing and giving me encouragement to do what fills my cup. Coming home from this conference I said to my husband, "I feel so inspired, I do not think I have ever felt like this before." I was thriving off all the positive energy from the kind words that were shared. I needed to go back to what it was I loved. Creating.

"What if I start a new business and the same thing happens?" I asked him. "I self-destruct the positive energy of new opportunities that are thrown in my path and struggle to take chances with fear of rejection, I am not sure I can do it again."

"Positive thoughts yield a positive outcome. If you think positive, positive things will happen," he said.

I wrote the phrase down on my vision board and any time I felt deflated I would read it to myself. It is so hard to change your mind set in such a short time when that is all you have ever known but I started to see results. It was only baby steps, but it was moving me forward in life.

I was just kicking off my new business and started to cold call potential customers to get my brand out there. This was really hard with so much rejection to the point I wanted to just give up. But at that moment I listened to that little voice inside that said, "Just one more call". I made another call and I gained some interest. I had someone interested in viewing my products and after meeting this client I made my first sale! My persistence had paid off. I did receive both positive and negative feedback. How hard it was for me to hear the negative feedback but I took it on board and made a few changes and turned that negative into a positive.

I noticed a real shift within myself. Implementing some positivity into my love for creating was so life changing for me. I always take any chance I get to go away with my family, camping in the bush, getting back to nature. With my boys getting more and more inquisitive about plants and animals I wanted to create a puzzle or game that would educate them. I had someone say to me, "Why don't you write a book?" I laughed. "Lucky if I got through school let alone become an author." There it was again—that negative mindset.

I asked myself, why couldn't I write a book? I already had the information so it was just a matter of putting it into a story. I was receiving so much inspiration from my boys and two days later at 4am, I woke and started to write. Before I knew it, I had written my first children's book based around my kids and exploring nature. I couldn't believe it! I had overcome that fear of not being worthy and believing in myself.

I read it to my husband later that morning and he looked at with watery eyes and a huge smile on his face and said, "You did it, babe, I am so proud of you." It was that very moment I thought, yes, I can do this. I wanted to show my creativity and passion without the negative influence and I could feel a shift. I had been longing for that encouragement for so long and all these years I had it all along. I had the family support I was needing, I just needed to open my eyes to what was in front of me.

I started to take every day as a new day. I stopped bringing in baggage from the previous day or any negative influences. I was loving my vibe, loving my job, loving my life, loved hearing other people's opinions and took them on board with a positive outlook. I was loving my new network of other business women I had met at the awards conference who were providing so much support and encouragement, something I had been lacking. With so much positive energy, most importantly I was gaining more confidence within myself and was in Love with the new me.

I had learnt to be more of a nurturing mother, becoming a positive and caring role model for my boys. I have realised with self-love and opening my heart I now have a stronger bond with my boys who have now become my inspiration which led me to become an author. I could see this starting to impact their life. They now fight over who will sit on my lap or next to me on the couch when we watch TV. It just feels right. It took me 40 years to get to this point in my life and I have now welcomed Love and positivity into all aspects of my life.

People think it takes a long time for people to change, but change happens in an instant. You need to do what fuels your desire to change, you must now recognise what it is you have and learn to embrace it. Before you attract what you want in life, you first need to give yourself the permission to do so. Learn to give love to help you receive. You must learn to remove negative people and surround yourself with loving positive energy. Let go of negative friendships and family to enable you to move on in a loving positive way.

Go where your energy flows, attract what you are, be grateful for the little things. If you do not appreciate the little things, you cannot accept the big things. You cannot love until you love yourself. You need to step outside to see what is within. No matter what you were told as a kid, you must love what you see. Do not let childhood experience define who you are. It all starts with self-love. Open your heart to who you are, who you want to become and who you want in your life. Ask yourself, who do you want to be? Learn to put ego aside, life is not about winning the argument, having to be right or having the upper hand. It is about putting love into everything you do and accepting every moment for what it is, opening your heart and letting it in. You do not attract what you want, you attract what you are.

About Karen Weaver

KAREN WEAVER is an award-winning publisher, author, TEDx Speaker and advanced Law of Attraction practitioner.

Author of numerous books across many genres, Novels, Motivational, Children's and Journals, she chooses to lead the way in her authorship generously sharing her philosophies through her writing.

Karen is also a sought-after speaker who shares her knowledge and wisdom on building publishing empires, establishing yourself as a successful author-publisher, and book writing.

Having built a highly successful publishing business from scratch, signing major authors, writing over 30 books and establishing her own credible brand in the market, Karen has developed strategies and techniques based on tapping into the power of Knowing to create your dreams.

Karen is a gifted teacher who inspires others to make magic happen in their lives through her 7 life principles that have been integral in her success.

When time and circumstance align, magic happens.

About The Alchemy of Life Magic Series

The Alchemy of Life Magic Series has been created to share the 7 core life principles of Karen Mc Dermott (Karen Weaver)

This series was born from the question Karen often got asked 'How do you do life?'

Her passion to share everything she learns on her insightful adventure of life has led her to share her 7 life principles of Mindfulness, Knowing, Intention, Love, Gratitude, Forgiveness and Belief.

In bringing it one step further she has invited guest contributors into each of the books so that they can share each life principle in motion.

Karen plans to record a documentary of this series. The books and documentary are purposely delivered to help those who sleep awaken. Just like she did.

More books by KP Weaver to add to your collection.

Book 1

Book 2

Book 3

Book 5

Book 6

Book 7

Find out more and get your free meditations at www.kpweaver.com or click here:

References

- https://www.readersdigest.ca/culture/love-ancient-mythology/
- https://youtu.be/c5RT_I9pWBg
- http://www.society-for-philosophy-in-practice.org/journal/pdf/4-3%2006%20Amir%20-%20Plato%20Love.pdf
- https://en.wikipedia.org/wiki/Law_of_attraction_(New_Thought)

www.ingramcontent.com/pod-product-compliance
Lightning Source LLC
Chambersburg PA
CBHW051538010526
44107CB00064B/2770